Invitation to
LINGUISTICS

INVITATION SERIES

Invitation to Economics	David Whynes
Invitation to Linguistics	Richard Hudson
Invitation to Politics	Michael Laver
Invitation to Social Work	Bill Jordan
Invitation to Statistics	Gavin Kennedy

Other titles in preparation

Invitation to Archaeology	Philip Rahtz
Invitation to Engineering	Eric Laithwaite
Invitation to Law	William Twining
Invitation to Nursing	June Clark
Invitation to Philosophy	Martin Hollis
Invitation to the Sciences	Barry Barnes

Invitation to
LINGUISTICS

Richard Hudson

MARTIN ROBERTSON

© R.A. Hudson, 1984

First published in 1984 by
Martin Robertson & Company Ltd,
108 Cowley Road, Oxford OX4 1JF

British Library Cataloguing in Publication Data

Hudson, Richard, *19—*
    Invitation to linguistics. — (Invitation Series)
    1. Linguistics
    I. Title   II. Series
    410   P121

    ISBN 0–85520–665–9
    ISBN 0–85520–666–7 Pbk

Typeset by Katerprint Co Ltd, Oxford
Printed and bound in Great Britain by
T. J. Press Ltd., Padstow

To Gay, Lucy and Alice

Contents

	Preface	viii
	Acknowledgements	x
1	Introducing Linguistics	1
2	The Pleasures of Linguistics	18
3	Ordinary Language is Good	38
4	Things You (sort of) Know Already	57
5	Strange Goings-On in Language	78
6	Puzzles	96
7	Theories: Boon or Bore?	117
8	The Great Issues (Grey Tissues?)	131
9	Some Applications	152
	Further Reading	167
	Glossary	170
	Index	179

Preface

FOR NOVICES

This book is intended for readers who don't know what linguistics is, but would like to find out more. In writing it, I have tried to give a clear idea of what it is like to study linguistics – what kinds of activities you engage in, and what their respective attractions are; so you should end up, all being well, with a better idea of whether it would be a good subject for you. I have tried throughout to write in a simple way, with examples that are as straightforward as I could make them. I hope you won't jump to the conclusion that linguistics is all like this book: most of the things you do on a linguistics course are quite a bit harder, and some are very hard indeed, so your capacity for thinking would be stretched as much by a linguistics course as by any other subject in the curriculum. But I hope too that you'll have an idea from this book of the fun and excitement that students can experience in doing linguistics.

FOR ADVANCED STUDENTS

You may pick this book up in an idle moment, out of curiosity, to see how I describe linguistics. No doubt you will have your own views on the pros and cons of the subject after however many years' study you have put into it. You'll probably find that the course you followed emphasized some of the activities that I describe here at the expense of others, and you've probably already worked out for yourself how the biases of your course relate to the personalities of the teaching staff. All I can say is that's life, and since you have a personality too, it could well be that the biases of your course worked in your favour. If they didn't, bad luck – but at least this book may help you to sort out better whether to blame the subject or the teaching staff.

You may also find the book helpful if you're at the point in a course where you want to see how all those loose ends tie up with one another; a quick read through this book may help to make a few connections.

FOR INSTRUCTORS

You may know enough of my previous published work to know that I hold unorthodox views on a number of subjects. If you're worried that I may be using this book to propagate my pet hobby-horses and presenting them as the orthodoxy, let me reassure you. I have made a special point of trying not to offend my colleagues, in the belief that linguists who are at loggerheads on particular issues nevertheless have a vast amount in common. It is this common ground that I have tried to emphasize, though I have also explained that controversy exists and have even stated my own position on certain issues.

On the other hand, it is inevitable that you will say to yourself that this isn't the book you would have written if you'd been asked to do it. My choice of examples, and also my choice of topics in which to express interest, are a reflection of my personality and may not fit yours. The aim of the book is to encourage students to opt for linguistics, so if it works, you'll have a chance to teach students influenced by the book, and you can set things straight then. Then I shall just owe you a little apology for the mismatch between my book and your personality. If the book doesn't work, though, I shall owe all of my colleagues a very big apology indeed. . . .

Acknowledgements

I received extremely helpful comments from three of our students, all of whom read the complete first draft of this book near the end of their first year, when they were still able to put themselves back into that blissful state of ignorance that they enjoyed before they joined us. They were David Appleton, Charmaine Faulkner and Gary Holden. I also received expert advice from the editor of the series, Kim Pickin, and from an anonymous linguist whom she persuaded to read the manuscript. I should like to thank them all, and assure them that every one of their comments has led to some kind of change in the book.

The first puzzle in chapter 6, on Latin, is based on an exercise from R. W. Langacker's *Fundamentals of Linguistic Analysis* (New York, Harcourt, Brace, Jovanovich, 1972); and the second one, on Zulu,· is based on an exercise from H. A. Gleason's *Workbook in Descriptive Linguistics* (New York, Holt, Rinehart and Winston, 1955). These are both excellent books, and if you enjoy chapter 6, you'll find plenty more puzzles in them, though some will be beyond the novice. The dialogue on page 36 is based on one in T. Winograd's *Understanding Natural Language* (New York, Academic Press, 1972).

1

Introducing Linguistics

My aim in this book is to help you, the reader, to decide
whether linguistics holds anything of interest to you, so we
start with a rough definition of linguistics: it is the study of
language. I shall use the term 'linguist' to refer to people who
engage in linguistics in this sense and not in the other, more
popular, sense of a person who is good at learning and
speaking foreign languages. A useful name for this kind of
person is 'polyglot'. Many linguists are also polyglots, but we
shall see that there are many activities within the field of
linguistics for which it isn't particularly important to be a
polyglot. If you are yourself a polyglot, or would like to be
one, then it is almost certain that you will find a lot of
linguistics fascinating, but please don't give up if you aren't.
If you can read this book, you must know at least one
language, English, and I shall be able to illustrate most of the
points I have to make in this book by taking examples from
English. (I shall follow the general practice among linguists of
reserving *italics* for linguistic forms quoted as examples.)

Linguistics is generally classified as one of the social
sciences, along with sociology (the study of society),
demography (the study of populations), the more socially
oriented branches of anthropology, geography and psychology, and so on. Like many of these disciplines, it is mostly
taught at 'tertiary' level, so if you wanted to study linguistics
in Britain, for example, you would have to go to a university,

1

polytechnic or college of education to do so. (Broadly speaking, the same seems to be true of most other countries too, and there are some countries where adequate linguistics courses are hard to find even at this level.) However, as recently as 1970 there were hardly any universities in Britain where you could take a degree in linguistics, in contrast with the situation in the early 1980s, so it may be only a matter of time before linguistics becomes quite common as a school subject. Already there are a number of schools and colleges where linguistics is taught at sixth-form level (or even below), and the experience of teachers is that there is nothing about linguistics which makes it any more unteachable below tertiary level than a subject like mathematics. I shall assume in this book, however, that the linguistics to which I am inviting you is the kind of linguistics that you would be likely to find in a tertiary-level course, or in a book aimed at that level, rather than the carefully selected parts of the subject that might be taught at school.

What we can call 'modern linguistics' – the kind I shall describe below – stands at the end of a long tradition of the study of language, going back to the Classical Greeks of about 500 BC. For various reasons the Greeks were very interested in their language and developed a sophisticated analysis of it which later acted as the model for analyses of Latin and then of all the languages known to the Europeans influenced by Greco-Roman culture. This book is not the right place to look for a description of this long tradition of study, so I shall recognize its existence, express profound respect for the achievements of bygone generations – and then ignore it all. I shall also ignore the particularly impressive version of linguistics which flourished in the last century (though I shall mention its present-day manifestation in the historical study of language); and I shall ignore all the long grammatical traditions found outside Western Europe, notably those of the Arabs, the Indians, the Chinese and the Japanese. All these traditions are strictly irrelevant, however valuable they may be in themselves, since I am assuming that you want to know what linguistics is like now, as practised in a typical department of linguistics (or 'linguistic science', or 'phonetics and linguistics', or 'general linguistics', or 'language', or . . .). This is what I shall call modern linguistics, or just linguistics for short.

This social and historical sketch may have started to help you to locate modern linguistics as a discipline, so we can now turn to its content. First I shall list some of the phenomena that linguists study, and then I shall say something about the ways in which we study them.

The best way to tell you what kinds of phenomena linguists study is to give you a list of the main branches of linguistics, with the names that are widely used for them. A three-year undergraduate course in linguistics is likely to cover most of these branches and may well be divided into parts so that each part deals with one branch. The list doesn't cover everything you might do in such a course – there are other branches of linguistics which deal with relations to other disciplines, such as the study of literature, which I shall mention briefly in chapter 9.

PHONETICS and PHONOLOGY deal with pronunciation. Phonetics studies sounds from the point of view of the physiologist (how we make them), the physicist (how the sound waves we produce differ from one another) and the psychologist (how we perceive them) but in each case, in principle, without much emphasis on the ways in which particular languages use the sounds. (For example, we might study the differences between vowels and consonants in these ways.) Phonology, by contrast, stresses this latter aspect and works out how sounds are used by languages (e.g. how different languages allow vowels and consonants to be combined with one another in different ways). Many practitioners feel that the boundary between phonetics and phonology is unclear and unimportant.

MORPHOLOGY and SYNTAX deal with words. Morphology concentrates on the internal structures of words – how they are made up from smaller parts, as *dogs* consists of *dog* plus *-s* – whereas syntax concentrates on the relations between words in a sentence (which are often called CONSTRUCTIONS). For example, in *Boys like girls*, it is morphology that discusses the fact that *-s* is added to *boy* and *girl* to make each of them

3

plural, but it is syntax that allows us to analyse the sentence as consisting of a subject (*boys*), a verb (*like*) and an object (*girls*). (By the way, if any of this terminology worries you, and you find it hard to remember, you can always check the glossary at the end of this book, where I have tried to explain any remotely technical terms that I use.) Morphology and syntax make up a good deal of what you may think of as GRAMMAR, though this often includes parts of the study of meaning as well.

SEMANTICS and PRAGMATICS deal with meaning (though there's also a broader definition of pragmatics which makes it responsible for the whole of language use, including some parts of meaning). The parts of meaning that come directly from the meanings of the words and constructions themselves are the province of semantics, whereas the parts which come from the context in which the sentence is uttered are handled by pragmatics. For example, if you hear someone say *He likes her*, you immediately know that the 'liker' is a male who is neither the speaker nor the person spoken to and likewise that the 'likee' is a female other than the speaker and the person spoken to, and all this information is of the kind which semantics studies; but when it comes to identifying the particular male and female in question, you have to make use of knowledge that comes from outside the sentence itself, such as who has just been discussed in the conversation concerned. At this point the semanticist in principle hands over to the pragmaticist, but, as with the phonetics/phonology boundary, some people feel that this distinction is neither clear nor important.

PSYCHOLINGUISTICS deals with the mind and behaviour of the speaking, listening and learning individual. For example, when we are speaking, how do we plan what we are going to say? How come we sometimes end up saying the opposite of what we mean (e.g. *too big* instead of *too small*, or *open* instead of *closed*)? Why do we have to work so much harder to remember some words (e.g. *nasturtium*, for me at least) than others (e.g. *daisy*)?

SOCIOLINGUISTICS deals with individual speakers as members of social groups and asks questions such as why there is so much variation within and between groups, and what kinds of variation there are.

HISTORICAL LINGUISTICS is about changes through time; we shall have more to say about it later in this chapter.

TYPOLOGY studies the ways in which languages differ from one another, partly with a view to discovering limits to this variation. For instance, some languages are like English in having 'pre-positions', so named because they precede their 'object' (to use the traditional word for the word which belongs to the preposition; take *in London* as an example – here *in* is the preposition, and *London* is its object). Other languages have 'post-positions', which are like our prepositions except that they follow their objects. An example of such a language is Japanese, in which the translation of *in London* would be *London ni*. Most languages can be classified as either 'prepositional' or 'postpositional', since they contain prepositions but hardly any postpositions, or vice versa. The interesting question for a typologist is whether this distinction is related to any other distinction that can be made on the basis of word order (or anything else, for that matter); some recent studies have shown that there is indeed a strong tendency for a postpositional language to have its verb at the end of the sentence and its adjectives before its nouns (as in English but not in French).

This list of branches of linguistics should have done at least one thing: to dispel the idea that linguistics is only about grammar. It is true that grammar is an important part of linguistics, but we touch on many other things too, and I shall try to emphasize the breadth of coverage in the rest of this book by selecting examples from different branches. Now we can turn to the other matter, which is how linguists study these various things.

TIME: SYNCHRONIC AND DIACHRONIC

Linguistics is time-sensitive, in the sense that it makes a clear distinction (in principle, at least) between 'historical' and 'non-historical' questions. I have chosen to start with this point because I find that most candidates who apply to study linguistics in our department find it quite hard to imagine questions other than historical ones. Typically, when I ask why they are interested in linguistics they say that it is because they want to know about the origins of things – whether particular words, or whole languages, or even the phenomenon of language as a whole. Now, there is nothing at all shameful about such questions (called DIACHRONIC – in Greek 'dia' means 'through' and 'chronos' means 'time'), and there are a large number of highly respected linguists who devote their lives to trying to answer them. But there are a lot of other, 'synchronic', questions (SYNCHRONIC – less obviously, 'syn' is Greek for 'with') which make no reference to history and which are equally interesting (even, we find, to those of our students whose first motivation for studying linguistics was historical). Moreover, as linguistics is currently practised most attention is given to the non-historical type of question, so it is important for prospective students to know about these questions.

To illustrate the kind of non-historical question that can be asked, let us take a particular example from English: the 'apostrophe *s*', as in *John's book*. Non-historical questions about apostrophe *s* involve its relations with other things which 'exist' at the same time. The following are examples:

(1)   When do we write apostrophe followed by *s*, and when just apostrophe?

(2)   Which of the 's-type' sounds does the *s* represent? (Notice that in *John's s* is pronounced as though it were *z*).

(3)   What is apostrophe *s* added to? (Notice that it is not added directly to the noun in *the man over there's name*; if it could be, the form would be *the man's over there name*, which isn't allowed.)

(4)   Does apostrophe *s* have a meaning of its own? (You may think it means something like 'possessor', but it is hard to see any kind of possession in expressions like *John's arrival*.)

(5)   In what stylistic or other circumstances is apostrophe *s*

used before a verb with *ing* as suffix? (Compare *John's coming late was a nuisance* with *John coming late was a nuisance*; you may feel that one of these alternatives is more suitable for casual speech and the other for fairly formal writing.)

If we restricted ourselves to historical matters, we could not ask any of these questions, so one of the benefits of separating historical from non-historical is that it allows both types of question to be taken seriously. However, another reason is that it avoids confusion. The fact is that languages change (which is precisely why the historical approach is interesting), so if we want to know about modern English, it is pointless to ask how things were in Old English. For example, in Old English the ancestor of our apostrophe *s* was added directly to the noun, just like our present-day plural *s*, but we have just seen that our apostrophe *s* is very different from the plural *s*, in that it follows not only the noun but also any of the noun's modifiers. So if you start with a phrase like *the biggest boy in my class* and make it plural, you do so by adding *s* to *boy: the biggest boys in my class*; but if you add an apostrophe *s* to it, to make it possessive (for instance), then you add the apostrophe *s* after *class: the biggest boy in my class's name is John.* (You may have been told at school not to use such expressions, but you probably do use them.) If we mixed up the facts about modern English and those about earlier stages of the language, we should be in danger of total confusion – the apostrophe *s* must be a suffix like the plural *s*, but at the same time it must be quite different. It is because modern linguistics tries to avoid confusion like this that we say that it is 'time-sensitive'.

CORRECTNESS: DESCRIPTION AND PRESCRIPTION

The second quality of linguistics is that it is DESCRIPTIVE, in that it describes what is rather than saying what ought to be. With most things that linguists want to talk about, there is no problem. For example, in spite of the history of our apostrophe *s*, nobody writing about modern English would argue that the apostrophe *s* ought really to be added to the noun, giving expressions like *someone's else hat* instead of *someone else's hat*, or *the biggest boy's in my class name* instead of *the biggest boy in my class's name*. However, for most of its long history the study of language has been PRESCRIPTIVE, which means that its purpose has been to tell people what they should say (or write) rather than simply to record what people do say or write, as in descriptive linguistics. This has meant that discussions of language have tended to concentrate on places where there is a conflict between some kind of standard language (such as the written language of an earlier period) and everyday usage, thus ignoring most of the facts about both. You are likely to be very familiar with the modern manifestation of this tradition, school grammar, with its lists of 'common errors' (for example, you should write *the man whom I saw*, and not *the man who I saw*).

We shall look in more detail at the liberating effects of taking a descriptive approach to language (see chapter 3), but our present job is just to explain what modern linguistics is like, so we need not go into the advantages of the descriptive approach. It is important, though, to stress the differences between this approach and the views of language to which you are likely to have been exposed at school (unless you were fortunate enough to have had an unusually enlightened set of teachers). We have already seen one big difference, namely that a descriptive linguist pays attention to the whole of a language, in contrast to the selective coverage of more traditional prescriptive approaches. Another major difference is that descriptive linguistics is non-judgemental, in the sense that it does not make judgements about matters of correctness in those areas of a language where there is a conflict between alternatives.

For example, linguists may observe that there are two past-tense forms for the verb *do: did* and *done* (e.g. *He did it* or *He done it*). We can study the linguistic rules controlling these forms (e.g. *done* is never used as an 'auxiliary' verb even by those who use it as a main verb, so a person who said *He done it* would say *Did he come late?* and certainly not *Done he come late?*); and we can study the social circumstances in which they

8

are used (e.g. what kind of person says *done* and what kind says *did*?). But all this can be done without linguists ever saying which of the forms is 'correct', even though it will soon become clear that *done* is never used on its own as the past tense in the speech of highly educated people or in writing. The fact that *done* is typical of uneducated spoken language does not mean that it is incorrect in some absolute sense; all it means is that there is a difference between the rules of uneducated speech and those of educated speech or writing. This is an example of the descriptive approach of modern linguistics, and, as you may imagine, linguistics can easily arouse the suspicion that it is a 'subversive activity'.

GENERALITY: LANGUAGE AND LANGUAGES

A third quality of linguistics is that it is GENERAL, in that it aims at producing generalizations about language. At one level this means making general statements about a particular language such as English rather than compiling a list of unrelated 'points' about the language. For example, we could list all the words of English, together with their spellings (and pronunciations), in a dictionary without thereby exhausting all that can be said about their spellings and pronunciations. In addition to the facts about each separate word, we can make various generalizations, such as the rule that the only consonantal letter (or sound) that can precede a *t* at the beginning of a word is *s*. (Compare the ordinary words *sting* and *stay* with the impossible combinations *lting* and *rtay*.) It should not be necessary to justify the search for generalizations: provided a generalization is true, it is bound to improve the quality of the description of English because it makes relations explicit which would otherwise be implicit.

Having made a certain number of generalizations, it is often possible to repeat the process, at a higher level, by making generalizations about generalizations. For example, what we have just said about *t* near the start of a word is equally true about two other sounds: *p* and *k*. All three of them can be preceded by another consonant, but only if this consonant is

9

s, as witness *spin* and *skin*, in contrast with impossible combinations like *mpin* and *pkin*. Moreover, we find that *p*, *t* and *k* have something else in common: they are all what phoneticians call 'voiceless plosives', which means that they are made without any vibration in the larynx or 'voice' and that they involve a little 'explosion' or sudden release of air. We can formulate a more general rule subsuming all those we have already made: if a voiceless plosive is preceded at the start of a word by another consonant, that consonant must be *s*. This general rule in turn is subject to even more general rules (the sound *s*, which is voiceless, cannot occur next to a voiced plosive in the same word), and so on.

The complete set of general statements about a language is called the language's STRUCTURE, and modern linguistics is generally described as STRUCTURAL LINGUISTICS to reflect this enthusiasm for discovering the structure of each language. (The term 'structuralist linguistics', by the way, is used rather differently, as the name of one particular branch of modern linguistics; it is easy to be confused by the terminology.)

What I have said about the concern for generalizing is equally true of the historical branch of linguistics. This has implications for those students who come into linguistics with a lively interest in ETYMOLOGY, the study of the origins of words. A high proportion of our students have this interest, as do a lot of people, so they enjoy a diet of odd facts about words – for example, that *tariff* comes from Arabic, that *window* originally meant 'wind eye', that *wife* and *queen* both used to mean just 'woman', that *hundred* is derived from the same ancient word as the Latin word *centum* (and therefore our *century* and *centimetre*) and so on and on. Most linguistics courses do not provide instruction in etymology as such, since this tends to be too atomistic for the structurally minded linguist.

However, we can provide something else instead: we can show how changes in the forms of words can be explained by means of general rules. For example, it is not just the word *hundred* which is related to a Latin word starting with a *k* sound (spelt *c*) in Latin; the same is true of *have* (related to *capere*, 'to take') and many others, so we can formulate a general rule that if an English word starting with *h* is related to any Latin word, then the latter started with the *k* sound. Similar general rules relate English words to words in other languages (notably languages like German, to which English is particularly closely related), and they can make etymologizing even more interesting because they suggest otherwise unsuspected connections.

A further service which linguistics can provide for the budding etymologist brings us to another point about the generalizing tendencies of linguists: that the generalizations at which linguists arrive include some which apply to more than one language. So we can tell you not only what particular sound changes have led to the known connections between particular pairs of languages but also something about how sound changes in general work and what kinds of change are most likely. For example, there are some kinds of change that we should be very surprised indeed to find – such as a change which precisely doubled the length of every word in the language. Similarly, we can describe some of the main ways in which meanings of words change through time which could alert you to etymological connections that you might not otherwise suspect.

The hunt for generalizations about languages is not restricted to historical linguistics and is in fact particularly characteristic of non-historical linguistics. This is why we often refer to modern linguistics as THEORETICAL LINGUISTICS. This rather forbidding name reflects the fact that for many linguists the main aim of their work is to develop a general theory of human language, so that particular facts about particular languages will turn out to be special cases of more general facts about language as a whole. For example, I mentioned briefly above that a voiceless *s* sound cannot occur in English next to a voiced plosive in the same word; we can raise the discussion to a more general level by asking whether the same is true of all languages. If we find that it is, then we can say that in a sense we have found out why it is true of English: it is true of English because English is an instance of a human language, and that's the way human languages usually are. (Of course, we can then ask why human languages in general are like that, and we may well find some kind of explanation in terms of what is easy to pronounce, but that is another question.)

You may well be wondering by this point how linguists can make claims about all human languages. After all, there must be hundreds of languages, and no linguist could know them all, so how could we answer a question like the one I have just posed? If anything, you are probably underestimating the size of the problem, because most people are surprised to hear how large the number of languages in the world is believed to be – something around 4,000 to 5,000. The fact is that there is a genuine problem when it comes to making generalizations across languages, and all we linguists can claim is that we do the best we can to make them true to the facts.

As I mentioned earlier, some linguists are extremely impressive polyglots, so as individuals they are quite familiar with dozens of languages (incredible though this may seem to most of us). Moreover, there are quite reasonable grammars and dictionaries available for several hundred languages, so, given time, energy, dedication and good libraries, a single linguist can find out a lot of things about a lot of languages. Furthermore, when linguists publish their ideas, they will be read by other linguists who may know a different range of languages; and human nature being what it is, the second group of linguists will be quite keen to tell the first group if they have gone wrong.

What all this means is that we can in fact generalize about a wide range of human languages; and if we find that some claim is true of the hundred or so languages that we happen to have access to, then we may be fairly confident that it will also be true of the next hundred as well. Of course, there is always the possibility that the next language we look at will undermine the claim we are testing, but even then we shall be left with a very strong tendency, which is almost as good as an exceptionless law. In any case, the present trend of linguistics is towards increasingly general statements about language, and every linguist welcomes any generalization which throws light on a host of particular facts, provided he or she feels reasonably confident about the truth of the generalization.

OBJECTIVITY: SCIENCE AND HUMANITY

Our fourth, and last, characteristic of modern linguistics is that it is objective. We try to make claims which can be tested by other people and which do not rely on others having the same subjective impressions as ourselves. For example, I may think that *My daughter likes daisy chains* is a lovely sentence, but there would be no point in my quoting this as a fact in my work as a linguist, because other linguists could not check whether it was true – either as an absolute truth or as a fact about me personally. A prerequisite for objectivity in this sense is reasonably clear terminology, and one of the things which strikes newcomers to linguistics is the wild proliferation of terminology (of which I am inflicting very little on you). Most of this terminology is necessary if we take our aims seriously, however, because ordinary language simply doesn't provide the terms we need for talking objectively about language.

It is because of this objectivity, plus the descriptiveness and search for generality described above, that linguists often describe their subject as a science. In principle, what we are trying to do is to formulate hypotheses which others can test; and since there is the real danger of being refuted, any linguist whose ideas have not yet been refuted can enjoy the belief that they are in fact correct. Similarly, the student has the opportunity of learning ideas which have not yet been refuted and which may well be correct. Since the ideas may well be of an extremely general nature (such as the cross-language generalizations referred to earlier), there is no need for linguistics to be pedestrian and pedantically detailed, and the matters at issue may be of quite general importance and interest, as we shall see in chapter 8.

Alongside this scientific objectivity, however, linguistics has a further quality which is worth emphasizing, though it is not a matter of principle on which linguists insist: it is highly personal, in the sense that a good deal of basic data are available within ourselves. This is true simply because every one of us knows a vast array of facts about at least one language, so we can treat ourselves as authorities on this language. Thus if I were to ask you what the past tense of *go* is, you would be able to tell me without hesitation, and furthermore everyone who knows enough English to read this book would agree on the answer (in spite of the fact that the answer is highly idiosyncratic and not the result of applying some general rule for forming past tenses). So when we are talking about past-tense verb forms, we are talking not about something existing outside ourselves but rather about a part of our own mental make-up (which may or may not also be contained in grammar books, of course).

This being so, you are already in a position to test most proposed generalizations against at least one language; so if I suggested the generalization that no linguistic rule has exceptions, you would immediately be able to refute it by quoting the exceptional past tense form of *go*. Moreover, I shall show in chapter 4 that there are surprises in store for us when we start to explore the linguistic contents of our minds, so at one and the same time the personal nature of linguistic data puts you in a position of strength and makes linguistics into quite an exciting exercise in self-knowledge.

What I have just said about linguistics should suggest that it is likely to combine some of the attractions of the natural sciences with those of the humanities. This is an important point because we find that some of the most satisfied customers among our students are those who enjoyed natural science at school and appreciate a certain degree of rigour and objectivity. Unfortunately, our secondary education is such that those who study languages at sixth-form level are generally firmly on the humanities side and may even have an aversion to natural sciences; and it is naturally from such a background that many of our students come, given the obvious connection between the study of languages and linguistics. A student with this kind of background may well flourish on the contents of a linguistics course simply by making the most of the (many) parts of the course where rigour is not stressed too much, but it often happens that the peculiarly personal content of linguistics makes the rigour and objectivity more acceptable, and a student with an arts background may end up with quite positive feelings towards the 'scientific method'.

ARGUMENTS AND AGREEMENTS

This completes my brief sketch of what linguistics is like. The following chapters will fill out the picture somewhat by giving more examples of the kinds of question linguists ask and some of the answers they arrive at. There is just one more thing I should in all fairness tell you about linguistics before we go on. Modern linguistics is a fairly young subject for all its ancient roots, and its main period of expansion in tertiary education was during the 1960s and 1970s. Partly because of its youth, its content is developing fast, so that those who did courses in linguistics in the late 1960s and return to look at the subject in the early 1980s find that the landscape has changed dramatically: most of the issues that were being debated in those days are hardly mentioned now, and the 'big names' are mostly new as well. In most courses on linguistics you become aware of controversy surprisingly early on (our first-year undergraduates already know some of the main bones of contention). Most students find the debates stimulating, and it is probably a healthy experience for anyone to see academic controversy from close-up, as an antidote to excessive reverence for the 'experts'. Educationally, then, the existence of controversy as an unavoidable part of any course in linguistics is valuable, provided it is well handled by the teaching staff; but its existence has to be recognized.

However, I should like to end this chapter by emphasizing that there is plenty in linguistics which is not controversial, including most of what I have said in this chapter. I am in the unusual position of being able to prove that this is so because I carried out a survey of opinion among a large number of my colleagues in British linguistics in 1980, which was published in a professional journal (the *Journal of Linguistics*, vol. 17). The survey resulted in a list of no fewer than eighty-three substantial points, covering all major areas of linguistics, on which all these linguists agreed, so it is reasonable to assume that most other linguists would accept them too, though I can't claim that every one of the points would necessarily be acceptable to every single linguist.

The following five points are taken from the above list and constitute the section which I called 'The Linguistic Approach to the Study of Language'. They will serve quite well as a summary of what I have said in this chapter and also as a preparation for some of the things to be discussed in the next one.

(1) Linguists describe language empirically – that is, they try to make statements which are testable, and they take language as it is rather than saying how it should be. (In other words, linguistics is descriptive, not prescriptive or normative.)

(2) The primary object of description for linguists is the structure of language, but many linguists study this in relation to its function (notably, that of conveying meaning) and in relation to other psychological and cultural systems.

(3) Linguists construct theories of language in order to explain why particular languages have some of the properties that they do have. Linguists differ in the relative emphasis they put on general theory and on description of particular languages.

(4) An essential tool of linguistics (both descriptive and theoretical) is a metalanguage containing technical terms denoting analytical categories and constructs. None of the traditional or everyday metalanguage is sacrosanct, though much of it is the result of earlier linguistic scholarship, but many traditional terms have in fact been adopted by linguists with approximately their established meanings.

(5) The first aim of linguists is to understand the nature of language and of particular languages. Some lin-

guists, however, are motivated by the belief that such understanding is likely to have practical social benefits, e.g. for those concerned professionally with the teaching of the mother tongue or of second languages or with the treatment of language disorders.

2

The Pleasures of Linguistics

Now that you have some idea of the character of linguistics, we are ready to discuss the reasons why people enjoy doing it, so that you can decide whether any of these reasons are likely to apply to you. In this chapter I shall list some of the main attractions of linguistics – seven of them, in fact – and each of the following chapters will take one of the attractions and discuss it in more detail. I have adopted this organization for the book in the hope that it will be helpful to you as you consider whether linguistics is likely to appeal to you. However, I should point out that because of this organization the structure of the subject will not be presented clearly, as we shall jump around somewhat from one area of linguistics to another. If you want a clearer picture of the major divisions of the subject and of its main findings, there are plenty of other books which you will find helpful and enjoyable (see the final chapter, 'Further Reading').

Here is my list of the attractions of linguistics. I am not claiming that all of them necessarily count equally with each of our satisfied students; on the contrary, it would be rather surprising if a student was equally keen on each of these aspects of the subject. In most courses there is sufficient flexibility for a student to choose the right balance for his or her interests and personality, and if you are thinking of applying to do a course in linguistics, you should make sure that you know how much flexibility is on offer. The following list may help you to decide where your own interests are likely to lie and therefore what to look for in departmental prospectuses and what questions to ask in an interview.

RULES ARE RELATIVE, SO ORDINARY LANGUAGE IS OK

In studying language objectively you become aware of how relative many of our rules are – that is, you realize that they are peculiarities of our particular language or community and that other people manage perfectly well with different arrangements. If we know of no alternatives, it is easy to come to the conclusion that the ways we have learned are in some way natural and inevitable, and this view is strongly reinforced by what we are told at school by teachers who often know little more than we do. To discover that other possibilities exist is for most students a liberating and enjoyable experience.

The most obvious sense in which linguistic rules are relative is that the connections between sounds and meanings found in words are essentially arbitrary, so there is no reason why we attach the meaning 'animal with a grunt and a curly tail' to the sequence of sounds *p-i-g* other than the (perfectly good) reason that this is what we found others doing in our particular community when we arrived on the scene, so we are simply following their example. There is a joke about a farmer leaning over a pigsty and saying, 'Rightly is they called pigs – they're such dirty creatures.' This man clearly believes that there is some natural connection between the sounds and the meaning 'dirty creature', so that his comment really does explain why we call pigs *pigs*; it takes a much more sophisticated awareness of the ways of the world to give an answer such as the one I gave above, which refers simply to the norms of our community. However, most students have this much sophistication, so I cannot claim that the point I have made here excites many of our students. It takes only a rudimentary knowledge of a foreign language to encourage awareness of the arbitrary connections between sound and meaning in vocabulary.

However, there are other areas of language where it is less

obvious how relative our norms are. Take the matter of pronunciation. It is common for educated English people to frown on what is called 'dropping' of the sound *h*, as in the pronunciation of the word *hear* which makes it indistinguishable from *ear*. Those who talk about *h*-dropping are quite clear in their own minds about what is happening: some people are careless and drop *h*s in their speech in just the same way as a careless knitter drops stitches. If such people were to pull up their linguistic socks and try a bit harder, they would be able to produce *h* where necessary.

There are two crucial facts that such experts on *h*-dropping ignore, one because they do not know it, the other because they do know it but overlook it. The first fact is that people who drop *h* do so because they have grown up in a community where other people drop *h*; there are other communities in which equally uneducated speakers do not drop *h* – *h*-dropping does not occur in North American English or Scottish English, for example. The fact is that *h*-dropping is an innovation which probably dates back to about the eighteenth century and probably started in or around London. Some communities have been affected by it and some haven't, but there is no reason to suppose that the affected communities are composed of more careless people than the others; it is much easier to explain the differences by saying that communities are more likely to drop their *h*s if they are in close contact with the working-class inhabitants of London.

The other fact which is relevant to *h*-dropping is that those who condemn it most strongly probably themselves use a pronunciation in which it is normal to 'drop' another sound, *r*, except when this is followed by a vowel. For example, they probably pronounce the words *saw* and *sore* in the same way, without any *r* sound. This is exactly comparable with using the same pronunciation for pairs of words like *hear* and *ear*, especially since there are other English speakers who distinguish the words in their pronunciation (again, most speakers in North America and Scotland do pronounce the *r* in *sore*, as do many people living in England). It is obviously inconsistent to condemn *h*-dropping as careless but to practise *r*-dropping (and possibly even to feel superior to rural speakers who don't drop *r*!). The difference between the two cases is clearly only a matter of who happens to practise them: *r*-dropping is acceptable because it is done by the educated and upper-class; *h*-dropping isn't because it is associated more with the lower-class and uneducated.

I could go on to point out that *h*-dropping is completely normal and acceptable to all in France (where all *h*s were lost by a general sound change that happened many centuries ago), but I have probably made my point strongly enough already: both the practice of *h*-dropping and also its condemnation are characteristic of particular communities and reflect the norms and values of those communities. There is nothing absolute or inevitable about either of them, so we can say that we have shown them to be relative.

LINGUISTIC CONSCIOUSNESS-RAISING

I have already mentioned that most of the discussion of general points in a linguistics course is illustrated with examples from English; it is also true that many courses include an extensive exploration of English for its own sake (which may take the form of a course on the phonetics of English and/or on the structure of English as a whole). This means that a good deal of time in a linguistics course is devoted to exploration of a language which you already know very well. It may be your main language, or it may be a language you have learned after learning some other one; but either way you start off already knowing (in some sense of the word) virtually all the facts that will be discussed in the course. Consequently, the main achievement of the course will be to help you to become aware of the knowledge you already have and to study it objectively. Students generally enjoy this exercise in self-awareness, and it may be that it improves their ability to look objectively at other parts of their mental make-up, though this may be wishful thinking.

The point can easily be illustrated with reference to examples I have already given, such as the observation about *h*-dropping and *r*-dropping. If you are one of those who drops *r*, you were probably not aware of the similarities between this and *h*-dropping until I pointed it out to you. Going back to the example of apostrophe *s* in the first chapter, you were probably unaware of the important difference between the rules for positioning apostrophe *s* and those for the plural *s* until my discussion made you aware of it. And so on.

However, I should like to introduce another example to make you aware of the extreme subtlety and precision of the knowledge at your disposal (if you are a native speaker of English; non-native speakers may not already know the facts I shall refer to below). The point of this example is precisely that it involves casual styles of speech furthest removed from the rather formal written styles which are discussed more or less explicitly at school; and because of this it is most unlikely that you have ever had your attention drawn to the facts I shall discuss. The example involves shortened forms of verbs like *will*, *is* and *have* (*'ll*, *'s*, and *'ve* respectively, as in *I'll see you tomorrow, John's here* and *I've finished*). For purposes of this discussion we can concentrate on just one of these verbs, *is/'s*, but what we say about this verb applies equally to all the others.

You may well believe that *'s* can replace *is* wherever the latter occurs, the only constraints being stylistic (i.e. you shouldn't use *'s* in certain very formal written styles; you may have noticed that I use forms like *'s* from time to time to show that I don't want my style to seem too formal). This is what linguists thought until someone pointed out an odd fact: in some sentences it is quite impossible to use *'s*, however casual your intended style may be. An example of such a sentence is *Mary is taller than John is*. There is no problem in replacing the first *is* by *'s*: *Mary's taller than John is*. This being so, we should expect that for consistency it might be better to do the same to the second *is*, but in fact this is impossible, as you will find (I hope) if you try to say the sentence *Mary's taller than John's*. Why is this? What we need is a hypothesis concerning the conditions for using *'s* which we can test, so let us explore a few alternatives.

First, we might think that the rule had something to do with euphony – that is, it is a matter of what sounds nice. Perhaps it is something to do with the juxtaposition of two consonants at the end of a sentence? We can refute this hypothesis immediately by making a minute change to our example: *Mary's is taller than John's* (referring, perhaps, to their respective fathers). This new sentence is completely acceptable (as you will find if you say it to yourself), but it ends in exactly the same sequence of sounds as the problem sentence, the difference being that in one case the *'s* is a shortened version of *is*, whereas in the other it is the apostrophe *s*. You can see, then, that whatever rule we come up with must distinguish between the *'s* corresponding to *is* and other forms which sound alike but are grammatically different.

For our second attempt we can try a hypothesis which does make this distinction: if *'s* is a verb, it must not occur at the end of a sentence. According to this hypothesis, the verb *'s* should be all right in the middle of a sentence, irrespective of what follows it. We have already seen one example of *'s* occurring comfortably in the middle of a sentence (*John's here*), but unfortunately there are other examples where something is wrong – compare, for instance, *Mary is unbearable in the morning, and John is in the evening* with the same sentence containing *'s* instead of *is* in the second clause: *Mary's unbearable in the morning* (so far, so good), *and John's in the evening*. The second *'s* here is just as bad as it would have been if it had been right at the end of the sentence, so the presence of *in the evening* after it can't be relevant, and the hypothesis we are testing must be wrong.

Our third hypothesis will fare better. Like the second one, it refers specifically to the verb *'s*, but this time it does not refer at all to the position of *'s* in relation to the end of the sentence. Instead, it refers to whether or not something is missing immediately after *'s* and says that *'s* is not possible if something is missing. Take our last example, *Mary's unbearable in the morning and John is in the evening*. Here something is missing after *John is*, namely the word *unbearable*. The fact that it is missing is easy to see from the fact that we all understand its meaning to be implied by the sentence – that is, *John is in the evening* means 'John is unbearable in the evening'. According to our hypothesis, *'s* should not be able to replace *is* in this sentence, and it can't. Similarly, *Mary's taller than John's* is impossible because there is something missing after *'s*, though it is not quite so easy in this case to see what is missing, since we cannot restore the missing elements without producing an unacceptable sentence (something like *Mary's taller than John's tall* would correspond to our interpretation of the meaning of the sentence). On the other hand, in *John's here* nothing is missing (because we can interpret this sentence without referring to any other sentence), so *'s* is possible. Our new hypothesis fits all the examples we have looked at so far – indeed, it fits all the examples that linguists have managed to think up during the last couple of decades – so we can take it as true.

What I hope this discussion has shown you is that any native speaker of English (such as you, if you are one) has a very detailed and sophisticated grammar of the language in his or her head, that this grammar has nothing whatever to do with the grammars that schoolteachers talk about and that it cannot possibly be connected with these precisely because we can be sure that few schoolteachers are sufficiently aware of this particular rule to tell pupils about it. So during this little exploration of a single rule of English grammar we have in fact been exploring the contents of your mind.

THE LINGUISTIC TOURIST

The third attraction of linguistics is the opposite of the second. Instead of making you aware of things which are extremely familiar to you, we can tell you about things that are decidedly unfamiliar and that will certainly strike you as very odd indeed. As I have already said, linguists try hard to formulate generalizations which will hold true about all languages, and we seem to have had a certain degree of success in doing so, which means that there must be significant similarities among the several thousand languages of the world. Nevertheless, differences remain, and during a course of linguistics you are certain to be surprised by what is possible in human languages.

Chapter 5 will be devoted to this theme, and we shall see there that enormous differences are possible between the structures of two languages. (Remember, the structure of a language is the sum total of all the generalizations we can make about it, including, among other things, all the rules of its grammar.) In one language the verb is the first word in its sentence, in another it is the last; one language uses ten words to express a message which another language can condense into a single (very long) word; one language uses the same case form (comparable with *I*, in contrast with *me*) for *John* and for *the dog* in *John came* and *the dog buried the bone*, while another language uses the case of *John* for *the bone* instead; one language uses different words for 'mother's brother' and 'father', while another uses the same word for both. The list is endless, it seems.

For the present, however, I shall take a completely different kind of example to show the limits of the possible. Instead of discussing language structures, I shall describe a particular social arrangement which has far-reaching implications for the ways in which people learn and use languages. The society in question is found in the north-west of the area that feeds the Amazon river, partly in Brazil and partly in Colombia; however, it is not the only instance of a society with the features I shall describe.

In this area there are about 8,000 Indians, divided into a number of tribes (apparently between twenty and thirty of them), which intermarry freely and consider themselves all to belong to the same cultural grouping. Now, there are two significant facts which make this society particularly interesting. On the one hand, marriage is exogamous, which means that a husband and wife must always come from different tribes; on the other hand, each tribe speaks a different language (language is, in fact, the main defining characteristic of a tribe). If we put these two facts together, it follows that every husband and wife must be native speakers of different languages. What is unusual, from our point of view, is not the existence of linguistically mixed marriages; we have all heard of such couples. Rather, it is that in the north-western Amazon area such marriages are normal, and in fact there would presumably be raised eyebrows if a marriage took place in which husband and wife spoke the same language natively, since this would mean that they came from the same tribe and would therefore technically be committing incest.

We can now add another intriguing fact about this society. There is a strict rule requiring the wife to live in the husband's family house and to speak his language, not only to him but also to their children. If we assume that in this society mothers play the same role in passing language on to the next generation as they do in our own society, then we have a situation comparable with every child in Britain learning English from a foreign au pair and not from a native speaker of English. It may be that this comparison is not in fact accurate, since the child in the north-western Amazon probably has extensive contacts with the other members of the father's family, proper native speakers of the father's language. Nevertheless, the differences between the contributions of mothers to language learning in the two societies are obviously considerable. One consequence of these differences is that a native of the north-western Amazon would presumably be puzzled by our use of the term 'mother tongue' to refer to the language one acquires first. He would wonder why we didn't call it instead 'father tongue'.

One benefit of learning about exotic arrangements like this one is that it allows one to reconsider one's own society, with the liberating effects we have already seen when we looked at the relativizing effects of linguistics. If we tried to see our own society through the eyes of a native of the north-western Amazon, we might observe some surprising things to do with language – such as the fact that people can be taken to court for using certain words (the so-called 'four-letter' words) in certain circumstances (publicly, etc.); or the fact that after many years of careful formal teaching of a foreign language we can still, to all intents and purposes, be mono-lingual; or the fact that each of us has two different names, according to who is naming us and when (e.g. I could be referred to either as *Dick* or as *Dr Hudson* in different circumstances, which need to be kept very carefully distinct if offence is not to be given).

STRETCHING YOUR WITS TO SHARPEN THEM

The next attraction of linguistics is that it makes you think hard by providing puzzles of all degrees of difficulty. If you do a course in linguistics, you will find that from time to time you will be given exercises consisting of problems to be solved (somewhat like the problems you had to solve in mathematics at school). These problems are generally selected so that they have a straightforward solution, and you will find them just as satisfying as you used to find those elementary maths problems. We often select data for the exercises from an exotic language, so that we can make sure that you have just enough information and not too much. (As we have seen, you already know a lot of facts about English, so if we set a problem from English, you could make use of facts other than the ones we had in mind, and these extra facts might confuse the problem in irrelevant ways.)

Here is an example of a baby-level problem taken from a language called Beja, a language spoken in the Sudan by nomads who live between the Nile and the Red Sea. (It is the language on which I wrote my Ph.D. thesis, so I shall mention it from time to time.) Your data are the following four one-word sentences:

1	tamani	I eat
2	tamiini	He eats
3	giigani	I walk
4	tamsani	I feed (someone)

Your task is to work out the Beja for 'He makes (someone) walk'. Try it first, before reading the next paragraph, bearing in mind that when you feed someone you are in a sense making them eat.

If you arrived at any answer at all, it was probably right,

and the way in which you tackled the problem is likely to have been along the following lines.

(a) Compare 1 and 2. They are partially similar in both meaning and form, so we isolate the similarities in both respects: they share the form *tam-* and the meaning 'eat', so *tam-* must mean 'eat'; therefore *-ani* must mean 'I' and *-iini* 'he'.

(b) Now bring in 3. Again we find *-ani* in the form and 'I' in the meaning, so our first guess seems satisfactory; *giig-* must mean 'walk'.

(c) Now add 4. This contains *tam-* 'eat' and *-ani* 'I', with *-s-* in between. It means 'I feed someone', which means roughly 'I make someone eat', hence the 'I' and 'eat' already identified; therefore *-s-* must mean 'make'.

(d) The Beja word at which we are aiming means 'He makes (someone) walk'. We know that 'he' is *-iini*, 'make' is *-s-* and 'walk' is *giig-*, so all we need to do is to put them together with *-s-* between the other two and *giig-* first: *giig-s-iini*.

Most of the problems that undergraduates are set are much harder than this, of course, and some of them are likely to contain enough material for several hours' solid work. As they get harder, the correct answers become less and less obvious, but in a well chosen set of data there will be a satisfying solution to the problem. These selected and limited exercises serve as preparation for the real thing, which is the solution of analytic problems which have not yet been solved by anyone. You may well have an opportunity to do this, under supervision, as some kind of project, and there is no doubt about the feeling of satisfaction you get when you arrive at a solution, knowing that you are the first person in the world to get there. I'm not, of course, suggesting that you will necessarily be able to solve problems that have defeated the professionals, but there are plenty of problems that are worth solving and have never been attempted by the professionals. And there is always a chance that you may notice a solution that hasn't occurred to the big boys; occasionally the journals carry articles by undergraduates who have done just that.

Problem-solving is a very important activity for under-graduates to practise, not only because it is fun, nor because there may be a remote chance of their doing research in linguistics after graduating, but simply because life is full of problems which need to be solved, and skill acquired in solving linguistic problems may transfer to other kinds of problem. Outside mathematics and the natural sciences there is on the whole not much opportunity for problem-solving at school, or in most undergraduate courses on the arts side, so linguistics can claim in this respect to offer a training that may well be valuable in later life. (I haven't yet discussed the ways in which the actual content of linguistics can be useful; this will come near the end of this chapter.)

THEORIES AS GLUE TO HOLD THE BITS TOGETHER

Another respect in which a linguistics course can be a satisfying experience is that linguistics can offer an overall theoretical framework which will help to integrate all the pieces of information you pick up in different parts of the course. I mentioned in chapter 1 that modern linguistics is sometimes called theoretical linguistics because of the need to assume some integrating theory when doing any work on the structure of a language. Once again, linguistics is rather favourably placed, certainly by comparison with the trad-itional humanities and probably also by comparison with many of the other social sciences, in being in a position to develop quite detailed and precise theories of the structure of its subject-matter.

The only problem, from the student's point of view, is that linguistics can offer not just one such integrating theory but a large number of them, since this is the area where controversy is most rife. Many departments help the student to cope with this problem by focusing mainly on one particular theory, at least at the start of the course, so that the student can become familiar with this theory before tackling alternatives. However, the experience of learning and evaluating more than one general theory is itself a valuable one if it helps you to cope with the wealth of alternative theories of politics, economics, religion and so on which confronts us all in our lives.

To make the discussion more concrete, consider one particular question of theory which arises in analysing the relations between the meaning of a word and its form. Take a word like *dogs*, which refers to many instances of the entity 'dog'; let us say that its meaning consists of two parts, 'dog' and 'many' (this analysis will do for the present, but it certainly wouldn't be good enough for a proper treatment). We can obviously also analyse the form of the word into two parts, *dog* and *-s*, so the question arises of whether we can establish a direct connection between each of these parts and one part of the meaning. We could represent this relationship in a diagram, like this:

dog ——————— 'dog'
–s ——————— 'many'

This diagram reflects one particular theory of this part of language structure, which we can call the 'direct form/meaning connection theory'.

An alternative to this theory would make use of the terms 'singular' and 'plural' to mediate the connection between form and meaning, so we could call it the 'indirect form/meaning connection theory', or the 'indirect theory' for short. An appropriate diagram would be this:

dog ————— singular ————— 'dog'
dog-s ————— plural ————— 'dog' + 'many'

The point about this diagram is that it shows that the unit to which we are assigning the meaning 'many' is the whole word *dogs* and not just the suffix *-s*. In other words, there is no direct connection between this *-s* and 'many, but one direct connection between *-s* and the label 'plural' and another between 'plural' and 'many'. Now, these two theories are different, and if we tried to avoid choosing between them while working on this part of the structure of English, we should almost certainly get into the most fearful confusion. So which do we choose?

There are a number of reasons for preferring the more complicated of the two theories, the indirect one, which is, incidentally, also the theory which is closest to the traditional treatments of classical and foreign languages (which do make use of the terms 'singular' and 'plural', of course).

First, we have words which mean 'many', although they do not contain a suffix like -*s*. One such is the word *people*, as in *People should be kind to one another*. If we say that 'many' is part of the meaning of a word only if there is a plural suffix, then we obviously can't say that it is part of the meaning of *people* (unless we resort to a trick, such as saying that there is a suffix which consists of nothing at all – an analysis without any obvious attractions); and yet we know that *people* does have 'many' in its meaning, just as *dogs* does, so something must be wrong. (Other such words are *sheep, fish* and *deer*; these have the same form in the singular and in the plural, in contrast to *people*, whose singular is *person*; but this difference is irrelevant here.)

Second, we find the reverse situation, where there is an -*s* suffix but 'many' is not part of the meaning. The word *linguistics* is an example of this (as witness *Linguistics is fun*, not *Linguistics are fun*). However, things are even more complicated than this because there are some words which contain -*s* and behave in some respects as though they did have 'many' in their meaning but don't in fact have it. Examples are *scales* and *oats*, which are just as single in their meanings as *balance* and *wheat* respectively but take agreement forms of accompanying words which otherwise are reserved for plural words – for instance, they take *these* rather than *this* (*these scales, these oats*, contrasting with *this balance, this wheat*). These examples are different from *linguistics*, which takes ordinary singular agreement forms (*this linguistics*, not *these linguistics*).

If we can refer to 'singular' and 'plural' as well as to the presence or absence of 'many', we can make all the necessary distinctions: *linguistics* is singular and not 'many'; *scales* is plural and not 'many'; and *dogs* is plural and 'many'. For distinguishing between words taking *this* and those taking *these* we simply refer to 'singular' and 'plural': *these* occurs with a plural noun (irrespective of whether this means 'many' or not). On the other hand, if we try to use the direct theory, without 'singular' and 'plural', we have no straightforward way to state the rule for choosing between *this* and *these* because we can't relate *these* to the presence of either -*s* or 'many' (in view of *linguistics* which has -*s* but doesn't take *these*, and of *scales* which lacks 'many' in its meaning but does take *these*). It seems, then, that we must prefer the indirect theory (a conclusion which most linguists would now accept, though at one time it would have been controversial). Using our diagramming method for this theory, we can show all the relations outlined above as follows:

dog ——————— singular ——————— 'dog'
dog-s ——————— plural ——————— 'dog' + 'many'
people ——————— plural ——————— 'person' + 'many'
linguistic-s ——————— singular ———————'linguistics'
scale-s ——————— plural ——————— 'scales'

What we have shown is that the indirect theory of the connection between word form and word meaning is better for English nouns. However, most linguists believe (to some extent as an act of faith) that if a theory is right, it should be equally true of all languages, so we should expect to find further confirmation for this particular theory from other languages – as we certainly do, though this isn't the place to demonstrate the point.

There are two consequences of assuming that linguistic theories apply to all languages. One is that we can build on a growing body of theory when we try to analyse a fresh language – we are not starting from scratch, in other words. For example, on the basis of the above discussion we should immediately look for mediating categories like 'singular' and 'plural' when dealing with word structure in a new language instead of trying to relate forms and meanings directly. The second consequence is that the theories we develop can be taken as theories of human language in general, so we may be able to relate them to other theories which apply to humans in general, such as theories of how we think or general theories about how communication takes place. These connections represent some of the 'great issues', which are our next topic.

The Pleasures of Linguistics

LIFE, THE UNIVERSE AND OTHER MATTERS

Most students enjoy thinking and talking about very general and important topics, such as free will, the place of women in society, the existence of God and so on. Some of the findings of linguistics lead into discussions of this kind and, not surprisingly, different linguists take different positions, so there is plenty to talk and think about if you enjoy operating at these heady heights. One of the main talking points at present is the question of whether or not human beings are genetically predisposed to learn language (in contrast to all other animals). The main advocate of the view that they are is the most famous linguist, Noam Chomsky; you may have seen him debating the point on television. However, I shall use a couple of other examples to illustrate the relevance of linguistics to great issues.

One big issue is about the relation between technological progress and linguistic change: as societies get more sophisticated, do their languages show a similar development from simple and primitive to complex and sophisticated? If they do, then it should be possible to take a grammar of a language like English or Russian, spoken by a sophisticated society, to compare it with a grammar describing the language of some very simple, 'primitive' society, such as an Australian Aboriginal language, and to find gross differences between the two. We have numerous grammars for precisely the kinds of language in which we are interested (namely, Australian Aboriginal languages), so what do we find when we make our comparison? The answer is very clear and decisive: there are no gross differences of the kind we might have expected that would allow us to look at a grammar of a language about which we knew nothing else and predict the kind of society which used the language. This conclusion is accepted by every linguist who knows anything about the languages of simple societies, though some nineteenth-century students of language thought otherwise.

You might think that there would be gross differences in vocabulary, if not in grammar, and that sophisticated societies would need (and would have) much larger vocabularies than more primitive ones. Just look at the half-million words in the complete *Oxford English Dictionary*, you say – how many hunter-gatherer societies can match that? The question is whether it is fair, or relevant, to compare the contents of a dictionary with the vocabulary available to a small tribe of illiterate Aboriginals. It would be much more relevant to compare the latter with the vocabulary of an illiterate group of people whose language is, say, English. It is very doubtful that we should find any appreciable difference in the size of the vocabularies of these two groups, so we can conclude that there is no connection between the nature of a society and the number of words known to its ordinary members, even if technology (such as publishing) brings with it the possibility of building up a large reference collection of words, of which no single speaker knows more than a fraction. I can again quote the results of my survey of professional opinion which I mentioned at the end of chapter 1: 'There is no evidence that normal human languages differ greatly in the complexity of their rules, or that there are any languages that are "primitive" in the size of their vocabulary (or any other part of their language), however "primitive" their speakers may be from a cultural point of view.'

A second issue to which linguistics is relevant is the question of the extent to which individuals are 'moulded' by their social environment. Here the answer is likely to be complex; it will probably amount to saying both 'a lot' and 'very little' at the same time. First, we can see in language clear evidence that people choose their models rather than being influenced equally by all the experiences to which they are exposed. For example, most British children spend a lot of time watching American cowboy films, but very few of them, if any at all, show any evidence of this in their pronunciation (except when they are pretending to be cowboys, of course). In other words, they choose not to follow this particular model as far as their own pronunciation is concerned. Furthermore, there is considerable evidence that we can shift from one model to another as the occasion demands (say, as between a chat with a friend at home and a formal interview for a university place). So to this extent we are very much in control of our behaviour and are not 'moulded' in a mechanical way by the society in which we live.

However, once we have chosen a model we conform to it in an amazingly detailed way and quite blindly. Consider your use of irregular verbs, such as *took* and *went* (past tense of *take* and *go* respectively). If English was the first language that you learned, then there was undoubtedly a period in your life (when you were about 4 years old) when you used regular past tense forms for these verbs (i.e. *taked* and *goed*), and it is unlikely that this presented any serious problem of understanding for those to whom you spoke at that time. However, I very much doubt if you ever feel any urge to use the regular forms nowadays, in spite of the rationality of doing so (you might see this as your contribution to tidying up the English language, for example). The reason is obvious: you would be laughed at or treated as an outsider by the rest of the community to which you belong, and this is a price that neither you nor anyone I have ever heard of would be willing to pay. Such conformity goes well beyond the needs of efficient communication and is motivated, apparently, only by the desire to be the same as everyone else, down to the finest detail.

It is particularly easy to study group pressures in language because the units of behaviour are so clear (e.g. different forms of a particular word) by comparison with other kinds of behaviour. It is debatable how we should generalize from language to non-linguistic behaviour and other matters such as attitudes and beliefs, but at least the question is interesting and important, and the light thrown on it by linguistics should make the discussion that much more fruitful.

LINGUISTICS CAN BE USEFUL

Last we come to the fact that linguistics can be useful, in the sense that it can help us to solve practical problems. There are a large number of ways in which linguistics can be useful, but we need consider only one of them here: the processing of natural language by means of computer, which will allow us to communicate with a computer without first learning a special computer language, such as BASIC or FORTRAN.

For example, it is already possible to conduct a 'conversation' with a computer about a limited domain of facts known to it, provided we are willing to apply the term 'conversation' to a dialogue in which both participants make their contributions in typed form. The following is a sample of dialogue between a user and a computer relating to an imaginary 'world' consisting of a number of blocks of various shapes and colours; such dialogue was already possible in the early 1970s, and much more sophisticated exchanges are now possible.

HUMAN USER	COMPUTER
Pick up a red block.	OK. [This means that the computer has carried out the instruction.]
Find a block which is taller than the one you are holding and put it into the box.	
What does the box contain?	OK. The blue pyramid and the blue box.
What is the pyramid supported by?	The box.
Can a pyramid be supported by a block?	Yes.
Which cube is sitting on the table?	The large green one which supports the red pyramid.
Is there a large block behind a pyramid?	Yes, three of them: a large red one, a large green cube and the blue one.
Thank you.	You're welcome.

This dialogue may strike you as pretty banale, but you will realize what an achievement it is as soon as you consider the detailed steps leading to any one of the computer's contributions. In order to make the dialogue possible, it was necessary to write a program which would allow the computer both to understand what the human user typed in and also to work out how to put its own answer into grammatical English. This would not have been possible without a sophisticated understanding of the structure of English, which came from linguistics. Furthermore, real breakthroughs in this area of computer science may well depend on our achieving breakthroughs in the understanding of language structure.

It should be fairly easy to see why progress in this area could be socially useful and important. If we could get our computer to accept any English sentence (or even 99 per cent of English sentences, with only one 'Sorry, I can't understand you' reply for every hundred sentences), then there would be no need to train users before they could use the system. It would be somewhat more of a problem to program the computer to express any message it wanted in acceptable English (the system which produced the above dialogue is very limited in this respect). Given a pair of programs for understanding and producing virtually any kind of English sentence, we could then provide computer systems for supplying vast amounts of information to users. For example, we could have a central store of information on all kinds of tertiary-level courses, so that you could tell the computer – without any special training, remember – what your interests and needs were, and the computer could advise you about where to go, what exams to take and so on. Furthermore, we should be a good deal nearer to the goal of translating by computer, something which is now considered feasible again, after a period of scepticism during the 1970s, partly thanks to new insights in linguistics. Numerous other computer applications to natural language are currently being investigated, and in every case linguists have an important contribution to make.

This completes my list of the attractions of linguistics. Each of the remaining chapters will explore one of these facets of the subject in more detail.

3

Ordinary Language is Good

WHY PEOPLE THINK ORDINARY LANGUAGE IS BAD

It would be a fairly safe bet that all the formal instruction about language that you have received since you started school has had two characteristics: it has stressed the things you don't know, and it has implied that there is just one standard of correctness. It all started when you were learning to read and write. At that time the only relevant skills were reading and writing, of which you knew nothing and the teacher knew everything; moreover, to all intents and purposes there was just a single standard of correctness, namely, the standard spellings given in dictionaries. As you got older, so the things you had to learn about your first language (such as matters of style) became more subtle, but the main problem was to teach you how to write successfully – with much less stress on speaking. Again the teacher knew it all, and you had everything to learn; and again there was a more or less monolithic standard of 'correct English' (avoiding forms like *I done it*) and 'good style'. True, the notion of a single standard has probably become more and more diffuse as you have learned about different kinds of writing, but the range of variation has remained very narrow. Meanwhile, you probably learned one or more second languages at school, and here too you obviously started with zero knowledge and were offered a single standard of correctness – any French sentence you produced was either right or wrong, and the notion that French actually shows as much variation as English does was kept very much in the background.

I am not criticizing your teachers for having taught you to read and write standard English or to speak and write the standard versions of other languages. If they hadn't done so, you wouldn't be able to read this book, and I take it that that would be a pity. The problem is simply that this kind of teaching is very one-sided and ought to be balanced by a different kind of teaching, one much more in line with the approach of linguistics. As I have already explained, linguists generally study ordinary spoken language rather than the more literary written varieties studied in school; and this means that a linguist could have explored the language you already knew before you started at school and revealed its increasing richness as you got older. By now you certainly know hundreds of constructions and thousands of words in whichever language you use for ordinary conversation (let's assume, for simplicity, that this is English); and you know many thousands of facts about these constructions and words, such as which ones are obscene, which are religious-sounding and so on. It is ludicrous to present the rules of standard written English without recognizing the prior existence of this vast store of information. Apart from any other objections, we could protest that the conventional approach to teaching about language flouts one of the golden rules of teaching, which is that the teacher should start from where the pupil is.

However, the problem goes deeper than this. For one thing, by giving explicit attention only to written standard English and to foreign languages we are implying that these are the only forms of language which can be studied explicitly; this may not be the intention, but surely it would be surprising if pupils didn't read this into the fact that teachers rarely discuss their language in the same way as these other forms. And, of course, linguists would reject this assumption in its entirety. In fact, some linguists would go even further and claim that ordinary spoken language is the most and not the least amenable form of language for systematic study. We shall see in the next chapter that there is plenty to study in ordinary language, including a mass of very precise rules which we all obey rigidly (for example, we say *five past six*, but never *seven past six*; we happily say *Try and come early*, but none of us would put this into the past, as *He tried and came early*). If one of the aims of education is to increase the pupil's understanding of him or herself, then we must count most language education as something of a failure.

Worse still, by giving attention to written and foreign languages we confer a status of respectability on them which, by contrast, we deny to ordinary spoken language. It is not just that ordinary spoken language is something we think we can't study, but also we are led to believe that it is not worth studying. This attitude contrasts markedly with the enlightened approach taken by many schools to other aspects of the child's day-to-day life, such as the local environment, domestic technology and so on. It is hard to think of any other part of a child's life which is denigrated in the way that ordinary language is. The result is that it is left to a course in linguistics to arouse any sense of wonder at the amazing achievement that every one of us accomplishes in mastering the intricacies of a human language.

All this is bad enough, but there is worse to come, as we all know. The unbalanced approach to language education does not just leave gaps in our understanding and miss opportunities for intellectual adventures. It also contributes to a range of social and personal problems to do with language. The implication of the usual approach to language education is that the written standard is the standard by which all language is judged; other kinds of language are judged as more or less deviant or 'wrong', according to how similar to the written standard they are. For example, in some parts of England the normal word corresponding to the standard *our* is *us* (e.g. *us books* instead of standard *our books*). Now, it would be quite possible for a teacher to call attention to this difference in exactly the same way as the French teacher would explain the relation between *notre* and *our*: 'If you're trying to use French/standard English, you must use *notre/our*; but of course if you're not, then *our* or *us* is fine.' This approach would probably be far more productive than the normal approach, which is to label *us* quite simply as 'wrong'. This blanket rejection of the child's normal language appears to offer a stark choice: either use *us* and be condemned for speaking bad English, or use *our* and be laughed at by your friends. Result: children opt for *us* and their friends but feel bad about their language. And, of course, things aren't improved when the teacher offers them explanations as to why they use *us*, referring to fictions like 'slovenly speech'.

To sum up, then: the little explicit comment that there is on ordinary spoken language is negative because it concentrates exclusively on those forms which are considered wrong, and unsystematic because it ignores the fact that any variety of language is a complex structure with its own rules. For example, take the past tense *done*, which I discussed earlier (as in *I done it*). If we simply label this word 'wrong' and tell the child that the correct form is *did*, we are ignoring the fact that the child already has *did* as past-tense form of another use of *do*, the auxiliary verb used in questions (e.g. the same child who says *I done it* would never say *Done I write enough?* but rather *Did I write enough?*). This essentially negative view of ordinary speech, to the extent that it is different from standard written language, involves whose who use this speech, in that the blame for the 'faults' is always put squarely on their shoulders. The implication is that if they pulled their socks up and tried a bit harder, they would be able to avoid the faults – in other words, if you use bad speech, it is because you are a bad person.

LINGUISTICS REACHES THE PARTS OTHER APPROACHES DON'T TOUCH

How does all this affect you, and how would you benefit from a course in linguistics? It depends, of course, on how non-standard your ordinary speech is. If you know that you use forms which some of your teachers wouldn't approve of, then linguistics ought to make you feel much happier about doing so because it will reveal your reasons (say, loyalty to your friends and family at home) and will show that there is in any case nothing inherently wrong with your forms – they are simply different from the standard forms, and it is only a historical accident that has promoted others to the status of standard rather than the one you use. If, on the other hand, your own normal speech is free of non-standard features, then linguistics should make you feel more charitable towards other people who do use non-standard features. Either way, the experience is likely to be important for you personally, as it will affect your view of your relations with other people and society at large.

There was a time (in the 1950s) when linguistics acquired a reputation for being on the side of total anarchy in language; in contrast to the rigid prescriptivism of school grammarians, linguists were supposed to believe that 'anything goes'. This certainly is not the view of linguistics that I am presenting in this book, nor was it really true of linguists in those days. What linguists say is not that it doesn't really matter what you say; rather, we claim that all varieties of language (including ordinary speech) are subject to rules, but that the rules for different varieties are simply different. The differences matter profoundly because we base on them all sorts of important social conclusions about other people – for example, if I hear people talking to friends and notice that they always use the full form of words like *not* and *is* (e.g. *That is not true* rather than *That's not true* or *That isn't true*), then I shall probably think they sound like pompous pedants and maybe even that they are pompous pedants. In other words, if you are trying to sound casual, then it is wrong to use nothing but full forms for words like *not* and *is* in just the same way as it is wrong to use short forms if you are writing something formal. In a nutshell, everything to do with 'right' and 'wrong' is important, and suitable for systematic study, but relative.

I should like to broaden the range of this discussion to include other kinds of language or language use which are often considered 'inadequate' and to show that linguistics has some light to throw on things other than non-standard dialect forms. We can distinguish four different types of 'inadequacy', including the one we have already discussed, to do with non-standard forms.

NON-STANDARD PRONUNCIATION

My discussion of non-standard forms so far has been over-simplified in one important respect, namely that I have ignored matters of pronunciation. The fact is that society at large recognizes some pronunciations as 'better' than others, and a child is just as likely to be criticized for using a 'bad' pronunciation of a standard word as for using a non-standard word. For simplicity we can talk about standard and non-standard pronunciations, but in the case of English the facts about pronunciation are more complicated than those which we have already considered because the standard pronunciation itself varies widely from area to area – one standard is recognized in England, another in Scotland, another (or rather, several more) in the United States and so on. This situation contrasts with other aspects of standard English, which vary much less from country to country, so that it is generally difficult to tell whether a piece of written English has been produced by an English person or an Australian, for instance.

The reason for the differences in status between alternative pronunciations of the same word (e.g. *house* with and without an *h*) is not the same as the reason for the status differences which we have looked at so far because they have nothing directly to do with the written standard. This must be so because, as I have just pointed out, 'standard' pronunciations vary from one country to another, so, for example, the standard pronunciation of *sore* is the same as that of *saw* in England but not in the United States (where the *r* in *sore* is pronounced). Furthermore, it is not generally true that standard pronunciations are nearer to the spelling than non-standard ones are. In some cases the standard is closer; in others it is the non-standard pronunciation which is closer. For example, in England there are non-standard pronunciations which distinguish words which are spelt differently but are not distinguished in their standard pronunciations. Thus the words *moan* and *mown* are the same in their standard English pronunciations but different in the non-standard pronunciations used in Norwich. (The literature is full of examples like this.) So we cannot say that if a standard pronunciation counts as 'better' than a non-standard one, this is because it is nearer to the spelling.

The explanation for status differences between pronunciations must lie elsewhere then. It is easy to see where if you have been brought up in a country such as Britain (or, to a lesser extent, the United States). Pronunciations act as symbols indicating the social groups with which the speaker indentifies. As I have already pointed out, no English child adopts an American accent as a result of watching American films on TV, and regional accents in Britain are alive and well in spite of the widespread use of standard pronunciations on British radio and TV. The reason is obvious: when children from Liverpool speak, they want to sound like Liverpudlians and certainly not like Americans. And, similarly, when people learn to 'talk posh' this is because they feel they can get away with passing themselves off as members of a higher social class than the one in which they started. The social pressures and choices which lie behind all these differences and changes in pronunciation are complicated and very powerful, but they can be studied systematically. And every one of us is locked into a system of social choices affecting pronunciation from which we cannot escape, though we can 'play' with the system in an impressively subtle way by using different pronunciations on different occasions.

People who grow up in Britain are probably more aware of the symbolic values of pronunciation than people in other countries, and we probably have correspondingly strong feelings about pronunciation matters; but what I am about to say could probably be matched by examples from most other countries. The problems that arise are rather similar to those which we looked at above when discussing things other than pronunciation, although the ultimate causes may be different. It is easy for people to conclude that if their speech is bad, they must themselves be bad people – especially if they are told that their bad speech is due to sloppy habits and insufficient effort. Worse still, they know that all the people with whom they identify socially use the same bad pronunciations, so they must all be bad; so the reason they themselves are bad is because they come from a bad group in society. Consequently, if they are to improve their speech, they must become better people, which means they must leave that particular social group.

The liberating effect of linguistics is to remove the value-judgements on the pronunciations so that you can look at your own speech, compare it with that of other people and notice differences without thinking in terms of which is 'better'. This still leaves the social differences between the groups which the pronunciations distinguish, but at least they are not reinforced by the supposed linguistic superiority of one group over another, so you should be less impressed by people simply on the grounds that they 'talk well', if by this you mean that they have standard pronunciations.

NON-WRITTEN STANDARD FORMS

We started off by talking about the way in which the written standard form is presented at school as the only variety worth considering, but we have now started applying the term 'standard' to matters of pronunciation. Here the relation of the pupil to the teacher is different, because the pupil does know how to pronounce (most) words, though he does not know how to spell any of them until he has learned this at school. What we are calling the 'standard pronunciation' is the one used by high-status (and typically highly educated) people; and as we have seen, this bears no specially close relation to the written form. We can now extend the meaning of 'standard' even further to include the ordinary speech of such high-status people, in contrast to the non-standard speech forms that we were talking about in the last section. The point I want to make here is that what is commonly called 'standard English' in this sense contains a lot of forms which would not normally be written and which suffer at school from the usual concentration on written language to which we have already referred. Once again, a course in linguistics helps you to appreciate these forms better and to see that many of the distinctions drawn between them and written standard forms are arbitrary.

One of the clearest instances of this is a four-letter word like *shit*, which isn't non-standard by our definition (because some of the 'best' people use it) but is definitely counted by most people as 'bad language'. It is written mainly in graffiti, which presumably get their emotive value from the fact that they infringe a very basic rule: when writing, you should use only 'good' language because written forms are (by definition) the standard by which we judge all other forms. The strength of the taboos surrounding such words is shown by the fact that we all know the words and what they mean, and yet many of us may never utter some of them throughout our lives, and if we have to refer to the thing designated by the word, we would do anything rather than use the word – even if it means using a technical synonym of whose pronunciation we aren't too sure (such as *defecate*). The objective approach encouraged by linguistics will allow you to explore all the taboo words you know, in a systematic and scholarly way, and to understand a little better the role they play in your life.

The four-letter words are the thin end of a very big wedge, commonly referred to by the very vague term 'slang', which would include expressions like *have a bash* meaning 'try' or *creased* meaning 'tired'. Since many of these expressions are longer and more complex than the corresponding neutral forms (compare *have a bash* and *try, go like the clappers* and *go fast*, and so on), there can be no sense in which we resort to them when we are feeling lazy, as an easy way out – again contrary to the impression given by some prescriptive commentators. So why do we use them? The answer must again be because of their symbolic value – presumably they symbolize our freedom from the written standard, since they are different from the ordinary forms. Consequently, we can use them to signal to each other that we are being casual and spontaneous, an important point when dealing with friends and other intimates. Furthermore, a lot of slang is what is rightly called 'teenage slang', used by teenagers to signal the important difference they see between themselves and older people. In this case the symbolic value of slang is like that of pronunciations, to which I referred above: it shows the social groups with which you identify (in this case a group identified not geographically but by age). Of course, each generation of teenagers creates its own slang to distinguish it from the previous generation (who are now the older generation), and each feels warmly attached to its own creation, so it is likely that you have your own favourite slang terms, which again you could study objectively as a linguist. However, you would find, if you did so, that from an objective point of view no generation's slang is better or worse than any other's, contrary to what you might expect (or hope) to find.

Even if we ignore such symbolically loaded forms as these (and there are plenty of other types within standard speech), there are still forms which are said but not written down and which are therefore never mentioned in school. An example is the range of very short questions which we attach to the end of a sentence, such as the *haven't we?* in *We've seen this film before, haven't we?* If I were to ask you what the rules are for deciding the form of such questions, you would probably not be able to tell me, though you would know that the form after *John will do it* must be *won't he?* and not *haven't we?* (as in the first example). A linguist could tell you the rules quite precisely and how they fit into your grammar of English, but you would be very unlikely to find any mention of this construction in any school textbook about English (unless, of course, you first learned English at school).

The point about all this is that linguists take seriously the parts of your language which schools never consider at all, and many of our students enjoy this experience, since it puts them (at last) in a position of strength in relation to language. As far as the basic data are concerned, any native speaker of English, above a certain age, counts as an authority, and all the linguist does is to systematize this knowledge explicitly. Students often find it hard to accept this reversal of roles, since they are used to being told by their teachers what is right and what is wrong in language; and when students are unsure about the choice between two forms they may still try to get the lecturer to adjudicate, authoritatively, even after several years of a linguistics course. However, it is a healthy change for students to be left, for once, without an authority outside themselves, so lecturers resist such pressures strongly.

Another advantage of taking ordinary spoken standard English seriously is that it should encourage you to use ordinary language when writing. For some people, the effect of what they learn at school seems to be that they feel that ordinary language can't be good enough for writing (otherwise the teacher would have paid attention to it), therefore it ought to be avoided whenever possible in writing. For example, you could write *Doing this made it easier for us to finish the job*, but this sounds too much like ordinary speech, so how much better to write something like *So doing facilitated our completion of the task*, which nobody would ever dream of saying? Verbiage like this seems to reflect a misguided conception of the relation between spoken and written language, and we should probably have less of it inflicted on us if our schools paid more serious attention to spoken language.

'LIMITED' LANGUAGE

Another way in which some people's language is often believed to be inadequate is that it may be seen as 'limited' in quantity. Some people (including many teachers) believe that there are children who have been brought up in English-speaking households but who reach school age without having acquired more than a rudimentary knowledge of English. They believe that such children (who normally come from relatively low-class families) have a very small vocabulary and only a limited range of sentence patterns. According to people who believe this, such children will turn into adults with comparably limited language unless the schools do something about it. Quite a bit of research has been devoted to this belief, and the conclusion is simply that it is false: all children (excluding pathological cases) have a large vocabulary, numbering thousands of words, and a complex grammar, by the time they are ready for school.

So why do some people believe the contrary? This is especially puzzling in view of the fact that many of them are schoolteachers and should know the children they are referring to pretty well. The answer seems to be that they judge children's knowledge of language on the basis of what they hear in the classroom, and there are certainly some children who are virtually inarticulate in the classroom, so the conclusion would seem justified if the behaviour of these children in the classroom were typical of their behaviour everywhere. But the classroom is in fact a very atypical environment for such children, and when their language in other, more familiar, environments is studied it always turns out that they have much more to say, and their language is as rich as that of other children who talk more impressively in the classroom. So we can reject the concept of speakers with very limited language in the same way as we rejected the concept of primitive languages (which would in effect be whole communities with very limited language). The problem seems to be the schools' – how to get these children to talk in school – rather than the pupils'.

This problem may be fairly remote to most readers of this book, but there is a related problem which isn't. When we consider the stated goals of school education (and universities too, for that matter), it is surprising how much effort is devoted to the (unstated) goal of increasing pupils' vocabulary. A lot of teaching involves the learning of technical vocabulary – *peninsula, equation, solution, mass, metaphor, sternum, noun, classical* and so on. No doubt this terminology is often necessary as a tool for exploring new concepts, but it can too easily turn into an end in itself (partly because it is easier to test knowledge of the term than knowledge of the concept). Furthermore, society at large sees a large vocabulary as a sign of the educated person, and a lot of people try hard to 'increase their wordpower' (as the 'Reader's Digest' puts it).

A moment's thought is enough to prove that the size of people's vocabulary, in itself, is fairly irrelevant as a guide to anything (except the effort they may have put into extending their vocabulary). If I know the word *hypothesis* and you don't, what does this show about the difference between us? It doesn't show that you lack a concept that I have because there is a perfectly good synonym, *guess*, which you presumably have, and (by definition) if it is a synonym of *hypothesis*, it must refer to the same concept. Nor does my knowledge of the technical term necessarily mean that I am any better than you at handling the concept (e.g. at formulating hypotheses, or testing them, or distinguishing them from facts). All it tells you is that at some point in my life I have read a book or attended a class from which I have learned the word *hypothesis*. Putting it rather crudely, a large vocabulary (especially a Latinate vocabulary) stands to education as cars and houses stand to wealth, in that it is the observable evidence which we present to the rest of the world to allow them to gauge the quantity of something which would otherwise not be observable (education/wealth). In this respect, vocabulary size is similar to accent, which is particularly closely linked with education in Britain (hence the term 'public-school accent' for the prestige pronunciation). It should be clear that there are more important things in education than acquiring the outward trappings of having been educated.

Another reason why you may have been under pressure to increase your vocabulary is that this allows you to satisfy two principles of so-called good style: to avoid vocabulary repetition and to avoid very general words, such as *get* and *nice*. The first principle (which I am violating by repeating the word *principle*, which I used in the last sentence) is meant to avoid monotony, but one suspects that it is also meant to encourage conspicuous display of vocabulary size. Likewise the second principle, though the purported reason for this is that words like *get* are so vague that you must be thinking unclearly if you use them. Therefore, you shouldn't say (or rather write) *I got a letter this morning* because what you mean could be put more precisely by *I received a letter this morning*. Of course, this is a very curious argument: if it is clear that you mean 'I received a letter' when you write *I got a letter*, then what is vague about *get* in this particular sentence? A short course in linguistics (especially the part dealing with meaning) is enough to show that it is quite normal for a large part of the meaning of a word to be supplied by the rest of the sentence, so what we should be evaluating is the vagueness of the whole sentence and not just of the word *get*.

The general conclusion to be drawn from all this is that the size of your vocabulary, in itself, is of no great importance except within an education system which values a large vocabulary for its own sake. It doesn't necessarily reflect the number of concepts that you have in your mind or the clarity with which you can use these concepts in thinking. If you worry about the size of your vocabulary, it may distract you from more important aspects of education, such as understanding the connections between concepts.

SLIPS

The last kind of 'inadequate' language is different from the other three: it definitely exists, and it is definitely inadequate in the sense of wrong. However, we shall see that linguistics once again takes a positive view of the inadequacy. What we have to deal with here are slips of the tongue, which are of great interest to linguists and are often referred to affectionately in the literature as 'tips of the slongue' in recognition of one of the main types (the spoonerism). The reason why they are interesting for a linguist is that linguists would like to understand how our minds work when we speak, and slips of the tongue provide an important source of evidence. You could say that they happen because we are careless, and in a sense this is true: if we paid more attention to what we say, the slips wouldn't happen. But this explanation doesn't tell us why the particular slips that we actually find occur and not other kinds of slip. For example, spoonerisms like *tip of the slongue* are common, but complete reversals of words never happen, so we should be very surprised indeed to hear someone say *pills* instead of *slip*, for example.

Most slips are caused by the 'target' word getting mixed up in our minds with some other word. In the case of spoonerisms this other word is one occurring in the same sentence, and what happens is that the two words simply exchange their initial letters in our minds. The Reverend William Spooner was apparently especially prone to producing them (hence their name), and once told off a student for wasting a whole term by saying, 'You have tasted the whole worm'; on another occasion he said, 'You have hissed all my mystery lectures.' Now, the interesting think about examples like these is that they show that when the speaker utters the first word he must already know that he is going to utter the second word; so when Spooner said *tasted* he already knew that he was going to say *term*, starting with a *t* (though he in fact ended up saying *worm*, starting with the *w* intended for *wasted*). What this shows is that when we are speaking our planning of a sentence is well in advance of what we are actually uttering, and we plan even the pronunciations of words long before we utter them. If this is so, then it is hardly surprising if words occasionally get mixed up, because we have a very complex mental process to work through: we have a number of words in our mind, waiting to be pronounced, and we have to make sure that we utter them, and their respective parts, in the right order. What is surprising, rather, is that we do the job successfully so much of the time.

Other kinds of slip allow us to unravel other parts of the planning process. How do we arrive at the list of words which we are going to include in our sentence? For example, how did Spooner decide that he would (eventually) say *term*? Obviously, he had to select this word from his vocabulary, and he selected it on the basis of its meaning, as the word which best expressed the concept he had in mind. Sometimes this process goes wrong in interesting ways. Sometimes we select the word which expresses a concept very close to the intended one – say, its opposite (e.g. *close* instead of *open*); sometimes the word we select is similar in pronunciation to the one which actually expresses the intended concept (e.g. *absolute* instead of *obsolete*); sometimes we select two words which both roughly express the intended concept and blend them into a single word (e.g. *grastly* instead of either *grizzly* or *ghastly*). Each of these types of error tells us something interesting about the way our minds work when planning a sentence, and linguists are gradually developing a coherent picture of the general patterns.

The kinds of slip that I have been discussing here are all quite normal by-products of normal speaking, and you are likely to be as prone to producing them as anyone else. They are certainly nothing to worry about, and the training you would receive in a linguistics course would help you to look at them as a source of great interest (and amusement). Of course, there are more serious disorders of speech which are worth worrying about because they prevent a person from communicating normally. These are the business of speech therapists, and training in linguistics is just one part of the preparation for dealing with them professionally. We shall have a little more to say about this application of linguistics in chapter 9.

HOW LINGUISTICS HELPS

What I have tried to show in this chapter is how linguistics can make some worries about language look less serious by changing the perspective from which we view them. The main contribution that linguistics makes in this respect is to take ordinary spoken language seriously as a phenomenon worth studying systematically and in its own right. This allows you, as a student of linguistics, to see your own ordinary speech in a positive way, in contrast to the view that most of us learn at school.

I shall finish this chapter by quoting the relevant claims about language on which I found that linguists were generally agreed. I have grouped them roughly according to the way in which this chapter has been organized.

Ordinary speech as an object of study

Language is amenable to objective study with regard both to its structure and to its functions and external relations.

Spoken language developed before written language in the

history of mankind, and it also develops first in the individual speaker: moreover, many languages are never written. These facts lead most linguists to believe that in linguistic theory priority should be given to spoken language, and many linguists give priority to the most casual varieties of spoken language, those which are least influenced by normative grammar.

The amount of knowledge involved in mastering a language is very great, although its extent is masked from ordinary adult speakers for various reasons, such as the unconscious nature of much of the knowledge. Children normally acquire a high proportion of this knowledge before they reach school age.

Non-standard spoken varieties

Different varieties of language are often associated with different social statuses, whether these are the result of birth (e.g. sex, region of origin, race) or of later experience (e.g. occupation, religion, education).

The prestige of a variety derives from its social functions (i.e. from the people and situations with which it is associated) rather than from its structural properties.

There is no reason for considering the variety called 'standard English' the best for use in all situations.

Pronunciations which deviate from the prestige variety are generally learned from other speakers and are not the result of 'slovenly speech habits'.

English spelling does not reflect the prestige variety of pronunciation any more directly than it does other pronunciations, so it is no easier for speakers of the prestige variety to learn.

The variety of language which a speaker uses on a particular occasion serves as an indicator of the speaker's group membership and also of the speaker's perception of the type of situation in which the speech is taking place. A speaker's choice of variety is not wholly determined by social factors beyond his control but may be manipulated by him to suit his purposes.

54

Pronunciation differences are especially closely associated with social group membership differences, and consequently they are especially value-loaded.

Mere exposure to a model different from that of peers or parents will not in itself lead children to change their own speech; they must also want to accept the model as the standard for their own behaviour. Many people go on using varieties which they know are low in prestige, and which they believe are deficient, because these varieties are the only ones which they can accept.

Non-written standard varieties

Every society requires its members to use different varieties of language in different situations.

All varieties (including the most casual speech) are 'languages' in that they have their own rules and vocabulary and they are all subject to rules controlling their use.

All normal speakers are able to use more than one variety of language.

Standard English subsumes a wide range of varieties and has no clear boundaries *vis-à-vis* non-standard varieties.

Limited languages

No speaker uses speech equally fluently or effectively for all functions (i.e. for all purposes and in all situations). Skill in speaking depends in part on having the opportunity to practise speech in quite specific functions rather than on general linguistic ability.

A child's poor performance in formal, threatening or unfamiliar situations cannot be taken as evidence of impoverished linguistic competence but may be due to other factors such as low motivation for speaking in that situation or unfamiliarity with the conventions of language in such situations.

Individuals may vary greatly in the extent to which their vocabulary covers particular areas of experience and also in the overall size of their vocabulary.

It is very difficult to measure a person's vocabulary meaningfully, partly because of the difference between active and passive vocabulary, partly because it is possible to know an item but not every detail about it, and partly because it is possible to know more vocabulary relevant to one area of experience than to another, so that measures based on just one kind of vocabulary do not provide a sound basis for estimating total vocabulary.

4

Things You (sort of) Know Already

In this chapter I shall expand on two points that I made in the last one: first, that your ordinary language has a structure which can be studied with some interest; and, second that you are an authority on your language – in fact, you are the only authority as far as your particular language is concerned, since you are the only person in the world with precisely the range of rules and vocabulary that you have. Of course, I am not claiming that you could immediately sit down and write a complete description of your language – far from it; not even the most experienced linguist is yet in a position to do that because of various outstanding theoretical problems that arise. But with a little bit of guidance from me, you will be able to start to build up a picture of certain small areas of your ordinary language – enough, I hope, to whet your appetite for more.

However, there is a problem. If you are the ultimate authority on your language, it would be nonsense for me to try to point out to you facts about your language, simply because I don't know what all the facts are. It is very tempting for a linguist writing a book like this one to lay out the facts, as he or she thinks they are, and to hope the reader will agree; but I believe it is important not to do this for fear of slipping back into the bad old ways of prescriptive grammar, which allowed a self-appointed 'expert' to try to lay down the law. The course I have chosen is to build this chapter in the form of a questionnaire, in which each question asks you to supply some quite specific bit of information about your language. I will then try to help you to pull some of the threads together on the basis of the answers that you yourself have provided. Needless to say, I have chosen the questions in such a way that they should allow you to give answers, and to draw more general conclusions without too much difficulty, if my guesses about your language are correct. But it's quite possible that your kind of English lies outside the range with which I am familiar, in which case you may have difficulties, and I owe you an apology. In case you are interested to know what answers I myself would give, I have included them at the end of the chapter.

Unfortunately, I couldn't think of any way in which I could avoid tying this questionnaire quite specifically to English, although I realize that English may not be your mother tongue. If you have a different mother tongue, you may decide to skip this chapter or to try out your knowledge of English on my questionnaire. Ideally, you would have a comparable questionnaire dealing with your own language because it is only in this way that I could persuade you that you are an authority on it (in a sense in which you may not be an authority on any native variety of English).

The questionnaire falls into four sections, each dealing with a different part of the structure of your English: pronunciation, morphology (the part dealing with changes in word forms), syntax (the part dealing with the rules for combining words) and meaning.

PRONUNCIATION

Vowels

Varieties of English all have a large number of distinct vowels, for which the five vowel letters of our alphabet are insufficient, so combinations of vowel letters have to be used, like *ee* and *oi*. Different varieties have different numbers: how many does your variety have? Check your most natural pronunciation of the words in list 1 to see if any of them rhyme. For each pair that rhymes deduct 1 from 15 to give your total. This figure is likely to be an underestimate; in

58

particular, if you have no *r* sound in your pronunciation of words like *fire*, then you are likely to have four or five more vowels in words containing *r* in the spelling. In addition, you may have distinct vowels in pairs like *brandy/shandy, eight/late, soul/sole*. For each such additional contrast you should add 1 to your total. If you explore and listen to yourself, you may well be able to find contrasts other than those that I have mentioned.

LIST 1

kiss	puss (addressing a cat)	price
mess	fuss	choice
gas	brass	house
loss	fleece	goose
wasp	face	sauce

Vowel classes

In list 1 all the vowels occur in words consisting of just one syllable and therefore containing just one vowel when you say them out loud. All these words end in a consonant (two consonants in the case of *wasp*), but many of the vowels contained in these words can also occur in monosyllabic words which have no consonant after the vowel in the pronunciation. For instance, the vowel of *choice* also occurs in words like *boy*. Not all the vowels can occur without a following consonant in a monosyllable – for example, you will probably find that the vowel in your pronunciation of *kiss* does not occur in any vowel-final monosyllable. Which other vowels in your repertoire are restricted in this way? They probably have in common some other characteristic (to do with their length): what is it?

Consonants: sounds and spelling

The words *a* (as in *a pear*) and *an* (as in *an apple*) are collectively called the 'indefinite article'. A simple rule determines whether you use *a* or *an*: what is it? If you don't know, ask yourself which form is used before each of the words in list 2, and see if you can work out the rule.

cat	dog
elephant	ant
giraffe	cheetah
monkey	donkey
ox	albatross

Now use your rule for deciding which of the words in list 3 start with a consonant IN YOUR PRONUNCIATION.

umpire	union
university	youth
horizon	hopper
house	hour
human	hurry

On the basis of your answer to the last question, which letters of the alphabet are most likely to misrepresent your pronunciation when they occur at the start of a word?

Consonant clusters

Between the beginning of a word and its first vowel there may be one or more consonants. In this question we explore the possible combinations of consonant sounds in this position by concentrating on a subset of your consonant sounds. You probably distinguish the following six 'plosive' sounds: *p, b, t, d, k, g.* These sounds are made by stopping the flow of air completely, then allowing it to escape with a little 'explosion' – you can probably feel the air rushing out after the *t* of *tie* if you put your hand in front of your mouth. The sound *k* is written not only as *k* (e.g. *key, kiss*) but also as *c* (e.g. *cat, cut*), *ch* (e.g. *chemistry, chaos*) or *q* (e.g. *queen, quell*). These six plosives can occur in combination with other consonants at the start of a word, but not all of them occur in all combinations. One combination is after *s* (e.g. *spine*), another is before *r* (e.g. *prize*) and a third is before *l* (e.g. *play*). Decide which of these three combinations each of the six plosives occurs in, and fill in table 1. (I have already filled in the row for *p*, taking account of the examples I have just given.) Then use the 'generalization' row at the bottom of the table to make as simple a statement as you can about the plosives which are possible in each position (e.g. if they can all occur, put 'any').

Table 1

plosive	after *s*	before *r*	before *l*
p	spine	prize	play
b			
t			
d			
k			
g			
generalization			

The examples we have considered so far contain up to two consonants at the start of the word, but this is not the maximum. On the basis of your analysis in table 1 you should be able to predict the possibility of certain combinations of three consonants. For example, we know that *p* occurs before *r* and that it occurs after *s*, so we can predict that it will occur both before *r* and after *s* in the same word, i.e. as *spr-*. We can test this prediction by looking for examples of such words, and we find them – *spray, spread*. Now fill in table 2 by first ticking the 'predicted' column as appropriate and then trying to supply relevant examples in order to test the prediction.

Table 2

plosive	between *s-* and *-r*		between *s-* and *-l*	
	prediction	example	prediction	example
p	√	spray		
b				
t				
d				
k				
g				

If your predictions were all confirmed, then your generalizations about two-consonant combinations are sufficient to cover three-consonant combinations as well. But if some of the predictions were not confirmed, then you need to supply extra generalizations for three-consonant combinations.

Past-tense suffixes

The past tense of *walk* is *walked* (e.g. *I walked a mile*) and illustrates the regular way of 'inflecting' a verb (i.e. changing its form) to form the past tense: by adding a suffix, *-ed*. Similarly, the past tense of *beg* is *begged*, with the same spelling for the suffix (and doubling of the preceding consonant, which we can ignore). However, you will find that the pronunciation of the *-ed* in *begged* is different from that in *walked*. In *begged* the suffix is pronounced as *d* (the *e* being silent, of course), which is a 'voiced' sound (made with 'voice', or vibration of your vocal cords – you may be able to feel this vibration by putting your finger on your larynx or Adam's apple). In contrast, the *-ed* is pronounced in *walked* as *t*, a voiceless sound. A third possibility is illustrated by *waited*, where the *e* is not silent, and the *d* is pronounced with voice as a *d* sound. The question is, what is the general rule for determining which of these three pronunciations you use for the *-ed* suffix? The answer has to refer to the pronunciation of the sound before the suffix, so your job is to find out which sounds occur before each of these three pronunciations. To help you I have given a list of verbs ending in a variety of different sounds in list 4 and a table in which you can fill in your findings. You will have to be careful to distinguish between spelling and pronunciation (e.g. *laugh* ends in the same sound as *cuff* in spite of the spelling), and you should aim for a very simple generalization about the sounds in each column of the table.

Verb forms

We now turn to the question of the number of inflected forms that English verbs have. If you know any other languages,

Things You (sort of) Know Already

LIST 4

rip	watch	rove
wait	pull	rouse
bake	roam	rouge
laugh	rob	wage
bless	wade	pin
rush	wag	play

Table 3

sounds before -t	sounds before -d	sounds before vowel + d

generalization

you may like to stop and ask yourself roughly how many forms verbs have in them. Just one? A handful? Tens? Hundreds? Thousands? Any of these answers could be right, depending on the language or languages concerned. Your answer will even vary according to which particular variety of English you use, and you probably don't know the answer without working it out, so this is what you will have to do. In the sentences in list 5 I have left blanks in which you can insert the form of the verb *talk* which you would use in that sentence – for instance, standard English requires *talks* in sentences like 1, but some people use *talk* instead when speaking casually.

LIST 5

1 Mary ___ too much these days.
2 Those students ___ too much these days.
3 Last year, Mary ___ too much.
4 Last year, those students ___ too much.
5 Mary has already ___ too much.
6 Mary's private life is ___ about a lot.
7 Mary was ___ when I came in.
8 Mary will ___ to you in a minute.
9 Mary wants to ___ to you.
10 ___ too much was Mary's downfall.

How many distinct forms of *talk* did you use? Now do the same with *speak*, and compare the two answers. One of these verbs is regular, and the other is not: which is which?

SYNTAX

Verb classes

In *He has seen him* we call *He* the subject, and there are two verbs, *has* and *seen*. I assume that your form for the corresponding question is *Has he seen him?*, in which the subject *he* has been put after the first verb, *has*. Now, not all verbs can be used before the subject like this – in fact, very few can. For example, you can't change *He saw him* directly into a question by inverting *saw* and *he* to give *Saw he him?* (I assume this is true of your variety of English). The question is, which verbs do you allow to invert? Table 4 contains a list of verbs for you to test, and you can show which are invertible by putting a tick in the first column.

Likewise, some verbs can have the negative marker *-n't* added to them (e.g. *He hasn't seen him*), but others can't (e.g. you probably can't say *He sawn't him*). The second column in table 4 is for you to record your judgements on the possibility of *-n't*.

Third, some verbs have a weak form (such as the one I discussed in chapter 2), and others don't. For example, you probably have a weak form of *has('s)*, which can replace it to give *He's seen him*, but no weak form for *saw*. Use column 3 to show which verbs have weak forms for you.

Things You (sort of) Know Already

Table 4

verb	example sentence	1 invertible?	2 takes *n't*?	3 weak form
has	He has seen him.	√	√	√
has	He has brown hair.			
has	He has a bath on Fridays.			
had	He had seen him.			
is	He is working hard.			
is	He is tall.			
can	He can swim.			
will	He will swim.			
wants	He wants to swim.			
starts	He starts swimming soon.			
gets	He always gets beaten.			

Do you see any pattern emerging from your answers to table 4? Some linguists refer to verbs like *has*, in *He has seen him*, as 'operators', in contrast to verbs like *saw*. Can you complete the following definition of an operator? 'If a verb is an operator, then . . . . ' Now look at list 6 and decide which of the capitalized verbs are operators.

LIST 6

1 He DID try hard.
2 He DID (DONE) the job well.
3 NEED we go now?
4 He NEEDS to work harder.
5 He USED to work too hard.
6 He TENDED to work too hard.
7 He HAD to work hard.
8 He GOT to see the manager.

Do you think the class of operators could be defined by reference to meaning, in addition to the syntactic properties already referred to? (It's debatable whether the matter of weak forms is strictly syntactic, but the other two properties probably are.)

65

Verbs taking infinitives

Let us call *to go* an infinitive (following the grammatical tradition and some, though not all, linguists). Some verbs can 'take' an infinitive and other verbs can't in spite of having very similar meanings to the former. For example, you will probably find that in your English you can use an infinitive with *cease* but not with *stop* (e.g. *He ceased to be interested in his job* but not *He stopped to be interested in his job*, except in the irrelevant sense of 'He stopped in order to . . . '). This is an important fact, from the point of view of a general theory of language structure, because it shows that syntactic characteristics of words – how they can be combined with other words – are to some extent independent of their semantic characteristics, which have to do with meaning. It is also a surprising fact if you think of language as an instrument for conveying meaning. You can test this claim as follows.

List 7 contains some verbs (and verb-adjective combinations) in jumbled order, but each member of the list is particularly closely related in its meaning to one other member. You should pick out the pairs and write them opposite one another in table 5, one in each of the larger columns labelled 1 and 2. Having done this, you should ask yourself whether each verb (or verb–adjective combination) does or does not take an infinitive (e.g. does it occur in sentences like 'He – to study linguistics'?), and note the answer, by a tick or a cross, in one of the inner columns. You can then look at the contents of these inner columns and see to what extent semantically related words are similar in taking, or not taking, an infinitive. I have filled in *stops* and *ceases* as a model.

LIST 7

anticipates	is likely
ceases	is probable
claims	likes
denies	looks
enjoys	sounds
expects	stops

Table 5

1	infinitive possible?	2
ceases	√ ×	stops

Verbs taking optional infinitives

Pursuing the topic of the last question, we can ask a further question about verbs that can take an infinitive: is the infinitive obligatory? Consider *try*, for example. Probably you'll find that you allow *try* to take an infinitive, as in *I'll try to help you*; but you may well also find that you can leave this infinitive unexpressed but understood, giving *I'll try* (which you might say after someone has asked you to help him or her, with the meaning 'I'll try to help you'). The interest of these cases lies in the fact that once again the meaning and the syntax aren't quite in step: as far as the syntax is concerned, there is no need to have an infinitive, but the semantics requires the meaning of some infinitive to be supplied (because you can't just 'try' in the abstract – you have to try to do something, and this something is what the infinitive defines). However, this option of leaving the infinitive unexpressed is not available with all verbs; for me, at least, it isn't possible with *tend*, so I couldn't reply, *Well, he does tend*, in reply to a question like *Does John work too hard?* (In all cases I can get away with just the *to* of the infinitive, so I could say, *Well, he does tend to* – but that's a separate matter.) Your job in this question is to explore the distinction between verbs that take an obligatory infinitive (like *tend* in my English) and those that take an optional one (like my *try*). List 8 contains some verbs (in random order) which I can use with an infinitive; assuming that you too can use them with an infinitive, distribute them between the two columns in table 6.

LIST 8

agree	begin
cease	claim
decide	expect
happen	hope
long	manage
ought	refuse
seem	tend
try	want

Table 6

takes obligatory infinitive	takes optional infinitive

Pronoun forms

In this question you will explore a different aspect of syntax: how you choose between forms like *I* and those like *me* according to the word's syntactic relation to the rest of the sentence. (In some varieties of English the same form is used in all cases, so for these varieties the present question doesn't apply; you can still ask the question about your version of standard English, however.) We have already related this contrast to the difference between subjects and objects, which is a syntactic difference: *I* (etc.) occurs as subject and *me* (etc.) as object (and, in fact, as anything other than subject). What makes the contrast between *I* and *me* rather complicated and interesting is the way it is applied to constructions with *and*. For example, some people would say *John and me did it*, and others would say *John and I did it*; some would say *She helped John and me*, while others would say *She helped John and I*; but neither group of people would say anything other than *I did it* (never *Me did it*) or *She helped me* (never *She helped I*). So the presence of *and* is also involved, for some people, in the rule for choosing between *I* and *me*. To help you explore this area of your language, I shall offer you three different rules (each of which will produce a different pattern of use), and you will need to decide which rule applies to your contrast between *I* and *me*:

Rule 1   Use *I* for the subject (with or without *and*). Use *me* otherwise.

Rule 2   Use *I* for the subject, provided there is no *and*. Use *me* otherwise.

Rule 3   Use *I* for the subject, or after *and*. Use *me* otherwise.

You may find that you need a rule not included in this list, in which case you will need to work it out for yourself (and pardon my oversight), but more probably you will find that you fluctuate between two (or even three) of these rules, or even that you aren't at all sure what you do say, in which case you may find it interesting to listen to yourself to find out. Having done all this for *I* and *me*, you can apply the same questions to other pairs (*he/him, she/her, they/them,* and *we/us*). Your answers may not be the same for all pairs.

MEANINGS

Pronoun meanings

We continue with the exploration of pronouns started in the last question, but now we are concerned with their meanings. (For simplicity we can refer to each pair of forms just by giving the subject form, so *I* really stands for *I* or *me*.) What you will be doing is called 'semantic analysis', which consists in making explicit the relations between each word and the other words of the language, and also their relations to things outside the language. Pronouns are a convenient area to practise on because it is clear which 'things outside language' they refer to: the person speaking (the speaker) and the person spoken to (the addressee). If we represent the speaker by S and the addressee by A, then the meaning of each pronoun can be specified as some combination of these elements – one or the other, or both, or neither. This is what is traditionally called 'person', though traditionally the contrasts are given, rather unhelpfully, in terms of 'first', 'second' or 'third'. In addition to person, you will need to give two other bits of information about each word: its 'number' (singular or plural) and its 'gender' (actually, 'sex' would be a better name, and the gender classes should be called 'male', 'female' and 'neither'). In the case of some of the pronouns you will find that there is no restriction on some of these contrasts, so you should put 'any' – for example, *I* can be used to refer to a speaker of either (i.e. 'any') sex. You can use table 7 to lay out your analysis, following the model of *I* which I have filled in for you.

Table 7

pronoun	person	number	gender
I	S, not A	singular	any
we			
you			
he			
she			
it			
they			

Having analysed all these pronouns, you can ask yourself how you would apply the same kind of analysis to the use of *you* meaning 'people', which can be replaced, in somewhat high-flown style, by *one* (e.g. *You have to work hard to get a degree these days*). Bear in mind the possibility of using 'any' as an answer.

Neither

The point of the next question is to show that a lot of words have quite complex meanings, so that the fact that you use only one word to express this meaning should not lead you to think that the meaning is a simple one. Semantic analysis can illustrate this by showing the similarity between the meaning of word X and that of some obviously complex expression; if word X has the same meaning as a whole phrase, and the latter's meaning is made up of the meanings of all the words in it, then the meaning of word X must obviously be that much more complex than the meanings of the individual words in the phrase. For example, *ever* means the same as *at any time* (compare *Did you ever go to Paris?* with *Did you go to Paris at any time?*), so *ever* must be as complex in its meaning as these three words put together. Likewise, *never* means the same as *not ever* (compare *I may never go to Paris* with *I may not ever go to Paris*), so the meaning of *never* must be as complex as that of *not ever*, which must be as complex as that of *not at any time*. Now you can apply the same kind of analysis to the word *neither*, as in *Neither book gives the answer*. Find a series of words which has the same meaning as *neither*, in the same way as *not at any time* has the same meaning as *never*. You will probably find that the phrase you need is one which isn't actually permitted by the rules of English; this needn't worry you too much, since the main things we are interested in here is finding a measure of the complexity of *neither*, so you can say to yourself, '*Neither* means the same as . . . . . would mean, if . . . . . were possible.' List 9 contains some words which you will find helpful, along with some others which you won't, so you need to pick out the relevant words first and then work out how to put them together to get the same meaning as *neither*.

LIST 9

banana	the
not	which
of	try
by	any
two	my

Time and tense

We now turn back to the verbs which took up so much of our attention in the questions on morphology and syntax. In the morphology section we investigated the forms taken by past-tense verbs and the total range of verb forms which are distinguished. Let us assume that we can call some verb forms 'past tense' and others 'present tense', illustrated respectively by *walked* and either *walk* or *walks*. The question is, what is the difference in meaning between these two forms? Assuming that you discussed this matter at all at school, it is quite possible that you were given a very simple answer: the present tense refers to the present, and the past tense refers to the past. The fact that the same terms ('past' and 'present') are used to refer to the verb forms and to their meanings gives a clear impression that the relation between form and meaning is a very simple one and correspondingly uninteresting. However, I can easily show you that there is much more to the tense system of your language than that.

We can start by replacing the terms 'past' and 'present' in our discussion of meaning to make the analyses of form and meaning independent. What does 'present' mean? It means something like 'at a time including the moment of speaking', so if we use 'now' for 'the moment of speaking', and 'event time' for the time of the event being described, then we can replace the term 'present' in the semantic analysis by 'event time includes now'. For example, the sentence *I live in London* contains a present-tense verb, *live*, which describes the 'event' of my living in London at a time which includes now. In contrast, *I lived in London* contains a past-tense verb, *lived*, which describes the event of my living in London at a time which does not include now but precedes it. So we can replace the term 'past' in semantic analysis by 'event time precedes now'. (You may notice the similarity between this re-analysis of the traditional past–present contrast as it applies to meaning and the re-analysis on page 70 of the traditional 'person' contrast, which I replaced by a more complex structure referring to the speaker and the addressee.)

Your task is to decide to what extent a very simple view of

the relation between form and meaning is true, and it will be easier for you to do this now that we have made the semantic analysis clearer. As we have reformulated the semantic analysis, then, the view you have to consider is this: any present tense verb refers to an event whose time includes now (the moment of speaking); any past tense verb refers to an event whose time precedes now. To help you I have included in list 10 some sentences containing past- and present- tense verbs (in capital letters). You should aim either to replace the above statement or to add reservations to it.

LIST 10

(a) Present-tense verbs
1   I LIKE cherries.
2   I GO to work by bicycle.
3   Oil FLOATS on water.
4   You will have fun when you STUDY linguistics.

(b) Past-tense verbs
5   I LIKED cherries.
6   I knew you LIKED cherries.
7   If I LIKED cherries, I'd go out and buy some.
8   It's time you WENT away.

PULLING THE THREADS TOGETHER

I have had two main aims in this chapter: to give you a taste of the interest you can get from studying your own speech objectively, and to show you how much detail your language contains. In the course of the chapter I have made a few fairly general points about the nature of language structure – such as various observations on the relations between syntax and meaning – but these points are incidental to the main business.

The relevant extracts from my collection of points on which linguists are agreed are mostly to do with vocabulary and syntax. Here they are.

General

Although all speakers know at least one language and use this knowledge ('competence') in speaking and understanding, very little of their knowledge is conscious. Knowledge of structural properties (e.g. rules of syntax) is particularly hard to report in an organized way.

Vocabulary

The specification of a lexical item (i.e. an item of vocabulary) must refer to at least the following types of information: its pronunciation (and its spelling if the language is a written one), its meaning, the syntactic and semantic contexts in which it may occur, and how inflectional morphology affects its form (at least if it is irregular in this respect).

There is no known limit to the amount of detailed information of all such types which may be associated with a lexical item. Existing dictionaries, even large ones, specify lexical items only incompletely.

The syntactic information about a lexical item may be given partially in terms of word classes, some of which correspond to traditional parts of speech. However, a complete syntactic specification of a lexical item needs much more information than can be given in terms of a small set of mutually exclusive word classes like the parts of speech.

Syntax

The analysis of syntactic structure takes account of at least the following factors: the order in which words occur, how they combine to form larger units (phrases, clauses, sentences, etc.), the syntactic classes to which the words belong (including those marked by inflectional morphology), and the specifically syntactic relations among the words or other units, such as the relations referred to by the labels 'subject' and 'modifier'. (Inflectional morphology is the part of grammar which deals with things like the relation between *dog* and *dogs* or between *take* and *took*.)

Things You (sort of) Know Already

Although English has little inflectional morphology, it has a complex syntax (i.e. it is not true that 'English has no grammar'). This is true of all dialects.

Vowels

I distinguish 14 vowels in this list (with the same vowel in *wasp* and *loss*), but I also distinguish the vowels in *fear, fair, fire, fur* and *tower*.

Vowel classes

I allow any of the vowels in the right-hand list to occur in a monosyllable without a final consonant, but none of the left-hand list. Those in the right-hand list also at least seem to be longer than the left-hand list.

Consonants: sounds and spelling

I use *a* before a word beginning with a consonant, and *an* before one beginning with a vowel. Therefore *university* and *union* must begin with a consonant in pronunciation, though not in spelling, and *horizon* and *hour* must begin with a vowel in pronunciation. So the letters *u* and *h* are most likely to be misleading in relation to their pronunciation.

Consonant clusters

After *s-* I allow any of the voiceless plosives; before *r* I allow any of these consonants; and before *l* I allow any of these consonants except *t* and *d* (which are both pronounced, incidentally, with the tip of my tongue up behind my teeth, unlike the other consonants). These generalizations do indeed suffice to predict exactly the three-consonant clusters that do occur in my vocabulary: *s*, followed by any voiceless plosive, followed by *r* or *l*, except that *l* does not follow *t*: *spr, str, skr,*

75

spl, skl, but not *stl* (e.g. *spray, stray, scream, split, sclerosis*). Oddly, though, the last of these combinations doesn't occur in any word except the rather learned word *sclerosis*, so if I didn't know this word, I wouldn't have any examples of *skl,* and my prediction would in fact be wrong.

Past tense suffixes

The vowel + *d* pronunciation is found after a *t* or *d* sound (e.g. *waited, waded*); the *t* pronunciation is used after all voiceless sounds, other than *t*; and the *d* pronunciation after all other sounds.

Verb forms

I have four distinct forms for *talk: talk, talks, talked* and *talking.* For *speak*, I have five: *speak, speaks, spoke, spoken* and *speaking.*

Verb classes

If a verb is an operator, then it is invertible, and it takes *n't,* and it has a weak form. Of the verbs in list 6 the following are operators: *did* in 1 but not in 2; *need* but not *needs; used* (but only just).

Verbs taking infinitives

None of the pairs I can put together are the same with regard to their taking or not taking an infinitive, in spite of their similarity of meaning.

Verbs taking optional infinitives

The following verbs take an optional infinitive: *agree, cease, ought, try, begin, manage, refuse.* Again no clear semantic pattern seems to emerge.

Pronoun forms

I think I always apply rule 1.

Things You (sort of) Know Already

Pronoun meanings

we: S, plural, any; *you*: A, not S, any, any; *he*: not S or A, singular, male; *she*: not S or A, singular, female; *it*: not S or A, singular, neither; *they*: not S or A, plural, any. *You* ('people'): any, any, any.

Neither

'Not any of the two'.

Time and tense

Any present-tense verb refers to an event (e.g 1), a series of events (2) or a possibility of an event (3) whose time includes now, or to an event in a *when*-clause whose time is the same as that of the main verb (4). Any past-tense verb refers to an event whose time precedes now (5), or to one whose time includes now provided the main verb is past tense (6), or to a hypothetical event when introduced by *if* or *it's time that* (7, 8). No doubt these rules could be better formulated, but the point is that there is no simple relation between tense and time.

5

Strange Goings-on in Language

DIFFERENCES THAT GO DEEP

I have already mentioned that linguists put the number of languages in the world at somewhere between 4,000 and 5,000, so any course in linguistics should give you some idea of the range of variation among these languages. So far we have concentrated on English to show you that there is a lot to be learned about this one language with which you are familiar, but it would obviously be nonsense to build our general picture of what language is like exclusively on this one language. One of the most lively branches of linguistics at the moment is the one which deals with this question, and students often find it a very stimulating experience to have their linguistic horizons suddenly expanded by learning about the ways in which other languages can differ, often quite dramatically, from their own.

We shall see that the differences go much deeper than you might expect even on the basis of some quite scholarly discussions of language – including, probably, the majority of books on foreign languages for the novice. (You may, for example, have tried to use a book from the 'Teach Yourself' series in order to learn a language not taught at school.) The impression such books give is that languages all have basically the same kind of organization in terms of the categories needed for classifying words and their relations in the sentence – they all have the same range of different 'parts of speech' (noun, verb, preposition, etc.), the same range of grammatical relations (subject, direct object, apposition, etc.), the same range of grammatical contrasts such as tense, mood, gender, case and so on, and of course they all allow the speaker to express the same ideas. According to this view, the only differences that need to be discussed are the means for expressing these basic patterns.

In fact, of course, you quite soon realize when you are learning a foreign language that differences are more interesting than this. As it happens, the languages most widely taught as second languages in Britain and America – French and Spanish – are both different from English in some very important respects in spite of also being Western European languages, and if you are interested in linguistics, this may be partly because you have been struck by these differences.

To take a simple example, in both French and Spanish nouns are classified as either masculine or feminine, whereas there is really nothing like this in English. The more you think about this gender system (especially from the English speaker's point of view), the odder it looks. Such languages start with the male–female sex distinction that is applied to living things, which is a natural enough distinction to make (and which English usually makes in its pronouns, of course); then they generalize the distinction to include everything which they can refer to by using a noun, including inanimate objects like tables and mountains and abstractions like the weather and beauty, and they distribute these objects in roughly equal proportions, and quite arbitrarily, between 'sex' categories (which we now have to call 'gender', if sex is to mean anything); and then they apply this arbitrariness to the original set of living beings and allow some beings to be 'misclassified' (for example, the word for 'sentry' in French is feminine). Historians of the languages can explain to some extent how this curious state of affairs has arisen, but it still strikes English learners of French and Spanish as odd when they first meet it. Unfortunately, your French or Spanish teacher may not have presented the gender system to you as an oddity to be marvelled at but may have implied instead that this was the natural way to do things; and indeed it may have been slipped through in the guise of being the equivalent of the English sex distinction, which it is not.

DIFFERENCES THAT DON'T OCCUR

Anyone who is keen to find major differences among languages can find them easily, and there is no need even for wide-ranging research into exotic languages, as we have just seen. The chances are that what you already know of languages other than English would produce a host of examples like the one I have just given. How much more readily, then, you would expect professional linguists to be able to show that languages are different from one another, when they have access to literally hundreds from the farthest corners of the world. And it is true that linguists have discovered a quite bewildering range of possibilities.

But there is another side of the research which I must also stress: what most linguists are looking for is the limit to the possible variations. This is natural enough, since it becomes less and less exciting to discover differences as you find more and more of them; to keep one's professional interest alive it is important to start asking the opposite question (what isn't possible?) as well.

Apart from matters of personal motivation, there is an important reason for wanting to discover the limits of what is possible, which is that many linguists want to work out a general theory of human language as a phenomenon exemplified by all the particular human languages. Now, if all we claim is that anything can happen, this amounts to saying that no such theory is possible. (Imagine a 'theory' of the weather which amounted to saying that you can never tell what patterns of weather are likely because all kinds of weather are possible in all circumstances.) We shall discuss linguistic theories in chapter 7 and we shall illustrate there the kinds of theories linguists try to formulate, but they all require us to accept some kind of limitation to what is possible in human language, the differences lying partly in what the various theories allow in language and partly in the explanations they provide for the limits.

We can return briefly to our example of the difference between French or Spanish gender and English sex to see how linguists with time to spare and an interest in the subject would plan their work. They would first take a deep breath and plunge into the available literature on a wide range of languages to discover as wide a range of possibilities as they could. They would discover that some languages have grammatical devices (little words or 'affixes') for classifying things according to their shape (long and thin, flat and round, etc.) and that others have devices for classifying as human, plant, animal and so on. Other languages, they would find, have elaborate but rather messy systems of classification, according to which some classes make sense (e.g. they consist of nothing but tools), while others don't (e.g. they include huntable animals and fish; a few domestic animals – sheep but not goats; cannon but not guns; and some military vehicles – aircraft but not aeroplanes). This very odd grouping is found in an exotic language called English; it constitutes the set of nouns which have the same form in the plural as in the singular.

Our linguists would try to fit their findings into a classificatory scheme so that different languages could be assigned to different 'types', and they would classify all the languages for which they could find information according to this scheme to make sure it was exhaustive. All the time they would be on the look-out for possibilities which were imaginable but had not yet been found. For example, they might wonder whether any language showed a simple classification based on the distinction between 'to do with man' and 'natural' (so that 'boy', 'house' and 'dog' would fall into one class and 'river', 'night' and 'hyena' in the other). I myself know of no language that makes this particular contrast, but this may reflect my ignorance, so they would need to keep an open mind about its possibility; but as the list of languages investigated grew longer, they might get more and more excited about having discovered a (putative) new fact about language: no language makes the distinction. If the results did in fact suggest this, they would then want to ask why, which would probably be a matter for speculation but none the less interesting and important for that. I shan't try to develop this example any further, but I hope it shows that the negative result of failing to find something is in a sense more important than positive findings.

Having said all this, I shall ignore the importance of the limits to variation in this chapter and concentrate on showing how vast the differences can be. Part of the reason is that it is much easier to do this in the space available (and also with the knowledge I have), but another part is that you are more likely to find the variation interesting, as you probably already have the impression that languages don't vary in very important ways because of the widespread views which I mentioned at the start of the chapter.

The one way in which variation between languages is certainly not limited is with respect to the parts of language which can be different. In particular, major differences are possible in pronunciation and in meaning (as witness the examples of gender-type systems which I discussed just now) and in all the areas in between the two, notably syntax, morphology and vocabulary. This suggests an organization for the rest of this chapter similar to the one I adopted in the last chapter – according to these different parts of language. I shall take most of my examples from the language called Beja, which I mentioned in an earlier chapter. You will remember that it is spoken in the Sudan (and parts of Ethiopia), between the Nile and the Red Sea. It is classified as 'Cushitic', which means that it is related to most of the other languages in the Horn of Africa and probably also to the Semitic languages (notably Arabic and Hebrew). There is no written form, nor is it taught in school (so far as I know), so I had to work out a writing system for it when I analysed it for my doctoral dissertation, and this is the transcription which I shall use here.

PRONUNCIATION

Even if you don't understand a word of a language, when you hear it on the radio it may well strike you as particularly exotic because of the sounds that are used. For example, Arabic sounds strange to European or American ears because it contains, among a number of other 'odd' sounds, one which is often described in introductory books as a 'retching' sound, like a frog croaking. Objectively speaking, there is nothing mysterious about this sound – a phonetician could explain to you how it is produced, could give you a demonstration and could probably even teach you to make it yourself. Nevertheless, it strikes us as odd because we are not used to hearing it in English or in any of the other familiar Western European languages. Again, several languages spoken in southern Africa (including Zulu) make use of sounds called 'clicks', which aren't used as part of ordinary English as 'tut-tut', which you make by sticking your tongue However, some of the click sounds are in fact quite familiar because they are sounds we make outside ordinary language – for instance, there is the sound which is usually written in English as 'tut-tut', which you make by sticking you tongue up against the roof of your mouth, then dragging it away without breathing out. What is odd about languages that use such sounds is not the sounds themselves but rather the fact they they are used in words, just like our consonants such as *p* and *t*.

Beja is not particularly striking from this point of view, but it does make use of two sounds which are unusual among Western European languages: a *t* and a *d* made with the tip of the tongue turned back, like an un-rolled English *r* sound. However, Beja does sound peculiar to an English ear because of the ways in which it combines sounds which we ourselves use but according to different rules. One of the more noticeable features is the way in which Beja speakers use the glottal stop, which English speakers all use at the start of a word beginning with a vowel if this vowel is particularly heavily stressed. (Imagine the following conversation, with you as B. A: *I always clean my teeth after breakfast.* B: *Always?* You almost certainly started *Always* with a glottal stop.) In Beja this glottal stop is used not only at the beginning of words but also after a consonant, which makes the consonant sound extremely forceful if it already involves an 'exploded' release of breath. For example, the word that means 'now' is *t'a*, which sounds like the start of a forceful utterance of the word *apple*, with a *t* before the glottal stop.

Another non-English feature of the pronunciation of Beja is its use of pitch. In English the musical pitch of one's voice goes up and down all the time when speaking, but this is all a matter of intonation, a 'tune' superimposed on the words. This means that a given word or series of words can be said with a number of different tunes; so, for example, you can say the word *yes* with a falling pitch ⟍, or a rising pitch ⟋, or a fall which turns into a rise ⟍⟋ or a rise which turns into a fall ⟋⟍. As you will find when you say these different patterns to yourself, each tune expresses a different attitude. For example, the fall–rise expresses reservation in my kind of pronunciation, so I would probably follow *yes* with *but.* . . . (There are important differences in the ways intonation can be used, so this may not be true of your pronunciation).

In Beja, on the other hand, pitch belongs basically to the word itself, so that each word has its own tune, just as in English each word has its own pattern of strong and weak stresses (for instance, in the word *English* you have to stress the first syllable, and stressing the second syllable is just as wrong as replacing the last consonant by, say, an *f*). Take the word which means 'shell', which is *kl'oob* (again the ' stands for the glottal stop). In this word you have to have a high, level pitch on the long vowel (represented by the double *oo*). However, if we make it plural, to mean 'shells', the tune must change to a fall, although everything else stays the same. There is nothing quite like this in English – it is as though a change of tune were to change the meaning of *yes* from 'I agree' to 'I disagree'. Although English does not operate like this, many languages do (and even more so than Beja, in fact), and this discovery comes as a surprise to most English-speaking students.

MORPHOLOGY

The most obvious difference between English and Beja is the amount of information which can be conveyed by means of changes in the form of a word. In English a word never contains more than one affix indicating an inflection. (I am ignoring affixes such as the *-ify* on the end of *solidify*, since these are used for forming new items of vocabulary rather than for distinguishing different forms of the same item.) So once you have put a past-tense suffix on a verb (giving, for example, *walked*), there is no way in which you can build up this verb by adding more affixes. Moreover, we have very few distinct affixes, which means that we can't distinguish many forms of the same word. You probably found about five distinct forms for regular verbs in the exercise you did on this part of your English (page 63), and you will also find that you have just two forms for each noun (e.g. *dog, dogs*) and three for each adjective or adverb that has an inflected 'comparative' and 'superlative' form (e.g. *big, bigger, biggest*). That is the sum total of possibilities for the inflection of English words.

By contrast, Beja verbs (in particular) have a vast range of possibilities. First, there are straightforward examples of inflection comparable with those discussed above. A given form of a verb may contain more than one affix, and there is a wide range of contrastive affixes. For example, take the word *tamyaaneet*, which would be used to translate 'which they ate' in 'some food which they ate'. We can analyse this word as follows:

tam 'eat'
y   third person subject
aa   past tense
n   plural subject
ee   relative clause marker
t   feminine agreement with the word for 'food',
     which is feminine

A word with five affixes marking inflections is unthinkable in English but commonplace in Beja. Because of this, a given Beja verb will be able to appear in dozens of different inflected forms, in contrast to the five forms of an English verb.

Another difference between Beja and English lies in the places where the inflectional affixes can occur. In English we have nothing but suffixes (affixes added at the end of a word); in Beja there are not only suffixes (as in the example just given) but also prefixes. For example, a Beja verb is made negative by the addition of a prefix *ka-* or *baa-*, and there are even some verbs which use a prefix where verbs like 'eat' (quoted above) use a suffix. For example, the form of the verb 'drink', which is otherwise comparable with the 'eat' example, is *išribneet* (*š* stands for the *sh* sound of *shop*), which we analyse as follows:

i	third-person subject
šrib	'drink', past tense
n	plural subject
ee	relative clause marker
t	feminine agreement

Here the marker of the third-person subject (which shows that the subject is 'they', not 'you' or 'we') is a prefix, whereas in *tamyaaneet* it was the suffix *y*.

Beja even has some affixes which occur inside the root (called 'infixes'). Take a verb like 'drink', for example. The way to mark such verbs as being in the present tense is to insert an infix *an* between the first two consonants of the root. – that is, between the *š* and the *r* of *šrib*. At the same time the vowel between the second and third consonants changes from *i* to long *ii*, so the root, including the infix, is *šanriib* in the present tense. For example, to make 'I drink' we add the prefix *a-*, which shows that the subject is 'I', and get *a-šanriib*. The nearest English comes to this kind of pattern inside a word is in verbs like *take*, which form their past tense by changing the vowel; but verbs like *take* are irregular and therefore exceptional in English, whereas the pattern I have just described in Beja is regular and common.

All examples we have discussed so far have involved changes to the verb's shape which linguists would generally classify as inflection. In addition to these, however, there are others which are more like separate words, though there are good reasons for treating them as bits of the verb (for example, they have no independent pattern of pitches, as free words generally do in Beja). One such word-like affix is the pronoun meaning 'you' as the object of the verb. This is pronounced *hook* or *ook*, according to the other affixes around it, and is a suffix. For example, 'they saw you' is *rihyaanhook*:

rih	'see'
y	third-person subject
aa	past tense
n	plural subject
hook	second-person object

Another word-like affix means 'when' and is pronounced *hoob*. It is a suffix and requires the relative clause marker which we have already seen. (This makes sense because 'when I saw you' means '(at) the time when I saw you', which contains a relative clause.) The word for 'when they saw you', then, is *rihyaaneeookhoob*:

rih	'see'
y	third-person subject
aa	past tense
n	plural subject
ee	relative clause marker
ook	second-person object
hoob	when

Yet another of these words is the one meaning 'is', pronounced *u*. This can be added to the word I have just built up, to mean '(it) is (or was) when they saw you'. (This could be used, for example, in translating 'When I saw you was/is when they saw you'.) And then we could add to this the word-like suffix meaning 'since, because' to give the Beja translation of 'since it was when they saw you', *rihyaaneeookhoobuaayt*:

rih	'see'
y	third-person subject
aa	paste tense
n	plural subject
ee	relative clause marker
ook	second-person object
hoob	when
u	is/was
aayt	since/because

SYNTAX

In English objects follow the verb to which they belong, and relative clauses follow the noun that they modify. In Beja the opposite order is either normal or possible, so the order of words in the two languages can be precisely the opposite. For example, if we take the English sentence 'Buy calves that have not drunk milk', you can compare the order of words in the two languages:

aat	milk
širbaat	(having) drunk
baa–	not
kaay–	being (i.e. 'have')
–t	feminine agreement with 'calves' (i.e. 'that')
lagaat	calves
dilba	buy (command)

Beja word order isn't always just the reverse of the order in the corresponding English sentence, but the above example gives an idea of the extent to which word order can vary from language to language.

Another syntactic difference between the languages is that English sentences have to have a subject (unless they are commands), whereas the subject is optional in any Beja sentence. The form of the verb shows the person and number of the subject (also its gender, if it is third person singular), and if the context makes it possible to identify the subject on the basis of this much information, there is no need to give more. In English this is not so. For example, we have to supply some kind of subject between *when* and a verb, so we can't say things like *I heard her when came in*, even when the form of the verb makes it completely clear who the subject is (for example, if the verb is *am*: try saying *I am happiest when am working*). As we have already seen, there is no need for a separate word to express the meaning 'they' in a Beja sentence such as the one we used to translate 'when they saw you'. If you know Spanish (or Italian or Latin or Russian), this will have come as no surprise, since the same is true of those languages.

More surprisingly, there is no need for an object to be expressed either unless it is first- or second-person. Thus *rihyaan* can mean 'They saw him', 'They saw her', 'They saw it', or 'They saw them', depending on the context. Nor is there any need for a noun to be accompanied by a word corresponding to *a* or *the*, so the Beja form for *a man* is just the word which means 'man', *tak*; and the Beja for 'They saw a man' is simply *tak rihyaan*. Once again, we find considerable differences in the sentence patterns that different languages use for expressing the same meaning. Rather misleadingly, perhaps, we could summarize all these differences, and those that we included in our discussion of inflection, by saying that English uses far more words than Beja in order to achieve the same results.

MEANINGS

Some languages make it easy to express concepts which in other languages are at best very difficult to express. Take the English expression *wicket-keeper*: how would you translate this into French or Spanish (or any other language you know)? The best you could do would probably be to use the English word itself and add a footnote explaining the rules of cricket and what part the wicket-keeper plays. And of course we cannot assume from the simple fact that someone speaks English that he or she will automatically understand this word – an American would have much the same difficulties as a Frenchman. What the Frenchman and the American have in common is that neither of them is familiar with this particular bit of British and Commonwealth culture, so the example illustrates one of the main reasons why languages can express very different concepts: they can be associated with very different cultures.

A more interesting example of linguistic differences that are associated with culture involves kinship terminology – terms used for referring to people to whom one is related. Look at the following list of terms used in at least British and American versions of English:

A	father	parent	mother
	brother	(sibling)	sister
	son	child	daughter
B	grandfather	grandparent	grandmother
	grandson	grandchild	granddaughter
C	uncle		aunt
	nephew		niece
D		cousin	

As I have laid these words out, the pattern looks quite neat because the male and female terms are exactly matched wherever they are distinct. In fact the system is even neater than it appears because we can describe all the relations by referring to just three questions. Before I say what these are I shall have to introduce some terms for the two people involved in the relationship. We can call one the 'relative' and the other one the 'possessor' (for lack of a better term). For example, in *John's father* John is the possessor and his father is the relative.

The three questions are these:

(1) What is the sex of the relative?
(2) How many links are there between the possessor and the relative?
(3) What is the direction of each of these links? (The link with a father is 'upwards', the one with a brother is 'sideways', and the one with a son is 'downwards', if you think in terms of a conventional family tree.)

All the words in group A (father/parent/mother, brother/sibling/sister, son/child/daughter) refer to a relative just one link away from the possessor, and they can all combine with *-in-law* or *step-* to produce expressions like *father-in-law* and *stepdaughter*. (The term *sibling* is in brackets because it is really a technical term from anthropology rather than an everyday word, and combinations like *sibling-in-law* seem even more artificial than *sibling* itself.) Interestingly, this grouping is a matter of culture and not of biology because there are two biological links, and not just one, between the possessor and a sister or brother (a sister is a daughter of one's parent or parents). Within group A, of course, the words are distinguished partly by the sex of the relative and partly by the direction of the link, as explained above. If we miss *sibling* out, this leaves a convenient hole in the middle where we can show the possessor, so we can draw a diagram to show how group A fits together (see figure 1):

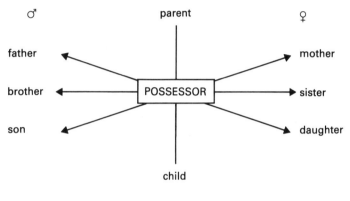

FIGURE 1

The next group (*grand-* combined with *father, parent, mother* and with *son, child, daughter*) involves two links between the possessor and the relative. For example, John's grandfather is the father of John's parent. In this respect they are like group C (uncle, aunt, nephew, niece), since John's uncle is the brother of John's parent, and his nephew is the son of his brother or sister. Both of these groups can be used with *great* (*great-grandfather, great-aunt*, etc.), showing that we are aware of the semantic similarity and reflect it in our language system. All the combinations of links that you could predict to be useful are in fact provided for: parent of parent, child of child, sibling of parent and child of sibling. All the other combinations are unnecessary in normal family circumstances – for example, the father of one's sibling is normally one's own father, and a sibling of one's sibling is

91

normally one's own sibling. We can add these two groups to the pattern for group A, giving another diagram (see figure 2).

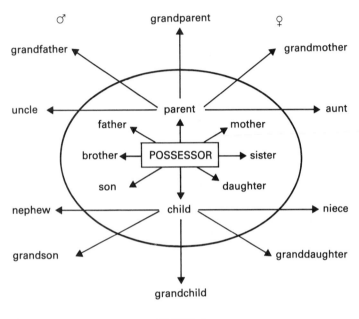

FIGURE 2

Last, we have the single word *cousin*, which involves three links between possessor and relative, so John's cousin is a child of a sibling of a parent of John. To add this to the above diagram we should need to have it in the centre of the page and linked upwards with both *uncle* and *aunt*, so I shall leave this to your imagination. You should notice, though, that the only kinship term that we have which does not allow us to show the sex of the relative is the one which refers to the most distant relative.

The main point is that we can describe all these relations by referring to just the three questions listed above: sex of relative, number of links and direction of links. Given the way at least a great many families in English-speaking countries are organized, this system makes a good deal of sense and can be described as 'natural'. For example, we treat people differently according to the number of links between us and them – we expect to live with the one-linkers (our 'nuclear family'), to spend Christmas, if possible, with the two-linkers and to keep in touch with any three-linkers who are within easy reach. And, of course, our behaviour towards relatives is heavily influenced by the direction of the links between us and by the relatives' sex.

It should be clear, though, that our kinship terminology is natural only in relation to our culture. Given a different kind of culture, we can expect to find a different system. In some cultures, for example, age is an important matter, so that younger brothers are treated very differently from older brothers and so on, and it is not surprising therefore to find that in the languages used in these cultures there is usually a different word for 'brother' according to whether the brother is older or younger. The difference between this kind of kinship system and ours is quite considerable, because as we have seen, our whole system of terms is based on just three questions; introducing a new contrast (age) at one point in the system is almost certain to mean differences in other parts of it too.

One of the strangest kinds of kindship structure is found in various societies which organize themselves into what anthropologists call 'moieties' for lack of any even roughly equivalent English term (the word is related to the French word *moitié*, 'half'). An example of a society organized in terms of moieties is the small Njamal tribe of north-west Australia. The arrangement that the Njamal make in order to avoid incestuous marriage is to divide the tribe into two moieties and to require everyone to marry someone from the opposite moiety. A person's own moiety is determined by a very simple rule: each child takes the moiety of the father. This means that a child belongs to the opposite moiety from its mother but the same one as the following people (among others): father; father's brother; father's father's brother's son; father's mother's sister's son; mother's sister's husband; and mother's mother's brother's son. One thing should be clear from this list: there is no English word that picks out all these relatives. But the Njamal do have a word for precisely this range of people, which (rather surprisingly) is *mama*, which is used to refer to any male who is just one generation older than the possessor and who belongs to the same moiety.

Once you know about moieties this terminology makes complete sense, just as the English system does when you know about our 'nuclear family'; and we could go on to analyse the sixteen words in the Njamal kinship vocabulary in just as systematic a way as we did with the English terms. But the main point I wanted to make with this example is that semantic analysis may require you to postulate some very strange concepts, when seen from our point of view. Conversely, of course, our terminology would no doubt strike a speaker of Njamal as very odd indeed because of the importance it gives to the number of links (something not shown in any way by the Njamal terminology).

I have saved till the end of this chapter my favourite example of an exotic linguistic phenomenon. One of the greatest linguists of the twentieth century, the American Edward Sapir, reported in 1915 that he had discovered the following facts about the Nootka, an Indian tribe living on Vancouver Island in British Columbia. Just as we have special ways of talking to small children (e.g. *doggy go bow-wow*), so the Nootka have special ways of talking either to or about various classes of people, namely children, unusually fat or heavy people, unusually short adults, those suffering from some defect of the eye, hunchbacks, those that are lame, left-handed persons and circumcised males. For each of these classes there is a distinct way of altering the normal form of a word in order to show that the speaker is aware of the physical condition in question.

For example, if a Nootka is talking either to or about a person who is fat or unusually big, he adds the affix *aq'* to the verb. (I shall use Sapir's transcription, in which *q* stands for a *k*-like sound made with one's uvula, and ' stands for a glottal stop.) This affix is put after the root but before some of the other suffixes, so that it is a genuine part of the verb and not just some kind of grunt stuck on the end. But, unlike the other affixes added to the verb, it does not contribute to the verb's meaning (at least not in the conventional sense of 'meaning') and does nothing but signal something like 'I recognize that you are fat'. Thus, take the one word which means 'He comes, it is said': this is *hint'ciLwe'in^i* (the little ^{i} shows a very weak *i* sound; *c* stands for *sh* in *ship*; *L* is a kind of *tl* sound), in which *we'in^i* means 'I am quoting somebody else'. To make this word suitable for using to a fat person, you add *aq'* before the *we'in^i* suffix, giving *hint'ciLaq'we'in^i*, which we can analyse as follows:

hin	vague verb stem, meaning 'be' or 'do'
t'	'come'
ciL	'starts'
aq	'you are fat'
we'in^i	'I am quoting somebody else'

If you were to do a course in linguistics or to read other books about the subject, one thing is certain: you would never come to the end of surprising facts about languages. After all, probably a majority of the world's 4,000 or 5,000 languages are still relatively poorly described, so we can expect a constant stream of new facts as linguists study the remaining ones. It would be remarkable if every one of these facts fitted neatly into the mould of what we think language is like.

6

Puzzles

Most of the working life of a linguist is a battle with language data of one kind or another, in which the linguist tries to make sense of the data, and the data behave rather like a mythical monster – as soon as you solve one problem, six more spring up to take its place. It is natural, therefore, that analysis problems should play a large part in any course on linguistics. They stand in the same relation to the training of a would-be linguist as does laboratory work to the training of a physical scientist. However, this kind of problem-solving is a fairly new and a valuable experience for most of our students, who typically have a background in languages or other humanities subjects. There is a good deal about data problem-solving that can be taught, but it is best taught in small groups where the instructor can interact with the students, so I shan't be able to able to teach you much in this chapter, but I will give you hints about how to tackle the problems I shall set.

Of course, the problems which you will find in linguistics textbooks and in problem classes are specially selected so that they work out more or less neatly, and you can be fairly sure when you have the right answer – indeed, some textbooks give a list of correct answers for you to check yours against (I give a list of answers at the end of this chapter). If you enjoyed maths at school because of the sense of statisfaction you felt whenever you got the right answer, then you will probably enjoy this part of linguistics too.

I hardly need to explain that real-life problems outside the classroom aren't generally as nice to the linguist as this. For one thing, textbook problems have all the relevant data laid out for you, whereas one of the main tasks of the working linguist is to bring together enough relevant data and to keep out irrelevant data. For another, it is common to find that before you can solve problem A you have to solve problem B and so on; textbook writers select their data carefully so that these additional problems don't arise. There is no need for me to apologize for the practice of textbook writers – if you take a linguistics course, you will probably be most grateful for their efforts to make your intellectual life tolerable – but you should remember that the real-life problems that linguists try to solve are much tougher than any you will come across in a textbook. This will help you to understand why linguistics appeals to people of very high intellectual calibre (not that everyone in linguistics is a genius – far from it – but there are plenty of clever linguists), and it may help you also to be more charitable towards linguists when you come to realize how many problems they still haven't managed to solve.

PROBLEM 1: CLASSICAL AND VULGAR LATIN

If you ever learned Latin, it is almost certain that it was the kind called 'classical', as written by famous Roman authors such as Caesar or Ovid. The kind of Latin which was spoken by ordinary people somewhat later is called 'vulgar' Latin (from the Latin word for 'crowd'), and it is from this kind of Latin that the Romance languages like French and Spanish were derived. The job facing us is to work out what changes Latin underwent in changing from its classical to its vulgar stages. (Actually, the relations between these two types of Latin are somewhat more complex than this formulation implies, but this does not affect the problem.) In particular, we shall try to work out some of the changes that affected the forms of words. For example, the classical form meaning 'donkey' is *ásinus*, where the accent marks the position of stress. (The notation we shall use is not quite the same as the traditional Latin spelling, which did not mark stress; the position of stress has had to be worked out by linguists, but we can be fairly confident of their guesses.) The corresponding vulgar form is *ásnos*, which is different from the classical *ásinus* in two respects: the *i* has disappeared, and the *u* has changed to *o*.

Now, we could 'solve' the problem by simply listing every classical word with its corresponding vulgar form, and we would in a sense have dealt with all the changes. However, I stressed in chapter 1 that linguists aim at statements that are as general as possible, and when we are dealing with changes between one stage of a language and another, we can expect to be able to formulate very general statements. What you have to do, then, is to examine the words in the pair of lists in table 8 and work out the general changes that took place between classical and vulgar Latin. You should be able to find six general changes, such that every difference in the lists can be taken as a particular instance of one of these changes. Having compiled your list, you will then be entitled to claim that you have explained why the words in the data changed in the ways they did: this happened because your general changes applied to any words to which they could apply. Of

Table 8

classical	vulgar	meaning
ásinus	ásnos	donkey
kálidum	káldo	hot
kéera	kéra	wax
kínerem	kénre	ash
díikere	díkre	to say
fúrnus	fórnos	oven
kolóorem	kolóre	colour
kírkulus	kérklos	circle
dúukere	dúkre	to lead
pílus	pélos	hair
stáare	estáre	to stand
stríktus	estréktos	close
spíina	espína	thorn
skúutum	eskúto	shield
plakéere	plakére	to please

course, this leaves you with your six general changes to explain, but at least you have just six explanations to find instead of fifteen.

One last note of explanation about the notation: a double vowel is longer than a single one, so the first vowel in *diikere* is (about) twice as long as the one in *Kínerem*.

Hints for working

You will probably need a pencil to do this exercise completely, and you may also find a separate piece of paper helpful.

Remember what you are looking for: six general rules which will account for all the differences between the classical and the vulgar word forms. At the end of these 'hints' I have provided a grid (table 9) for your six rules, with a space for whatever the relevant part of the classical form is and then another space to show what happened to this form in vulgar Latin. For example, if you find that all classical *p*s turn into vulgar *r*s (you won't, so I'm not giving anything away by this example), then you simply put *p* in the first column of the grid and *r* into the second. If something is lost altogether, just put a dash in the second column.

If you can go straight to the answer, do; you would probably find the problem-solving part of a linguistics course easy and enjoyable. If you have difficulty, it may well mean simply that you need some training in problem-solving. Try the following plan of attack:

(1) Take the first pair of words and isolate the differences. As we have already seen, there are two of them: loss of *i* and change of *u* to *o*.

(2) Assume provisionally that these two changes are among the six general rules you are looking for and write them down in the grid. (If you're wrong or they need revising, you can always change the entry – you're not aiming for a fair copy.)

(3) Now take the next pair and see if they involve any changes other than the ones you already have in your grid. If they don't, pass on to the next pair and so on. If

they do, you must adjust your grid either by adding extra rules or by making the rules you already have more general so that they cover the extra changes.

(4) Keep on repeating 3 until you have finished the list of words; by this time the grid should be full.

Table 9

	classical form	corresponding vulgar form
rule 1		
rule 2		
rule 3		
rule 4		
rule 5		
rule 6		

PROBLEM 2: ZULU VOWELS

In this problem we focus on part of the sound system of Zulu, which is spoken in South Africa. The sound system of a language is the set of sounds used in that language, plus the relations between them. What we often find when we analyse sound systems is that one sound may be regarded as a kind of deviation from another because of the effects of the contexts in which the former occurs. For example, try saying the word *emphatic* to yourself. You probably think the first consonant (after the *e*) is an *m* sound, but you are likely to have pronounced it with a different movement of your lips. Normally, you make *m* by putting your top and bottom lips together, but in *emphatic* you probably have your bottom lip touching your top teeth and not your top lip. The reason why this happens is simple: the *f* sound represented in the spelling by *ph* requires the bottom lip to touch the top teeth, so you start preparing for this position while you are making the *m* sound. To put this another way, you make the *m* more similar to the following consonant than it would otherwise be.

It is very common for sounds to be made more similar

(or assimilated) to their phonetic context than they would otherwise be, so an experienced linguist analysing data in a new language would be on the look-out for the phenomenon. Having found an instance of it, the linguist can do two things: write a rule to state the generalization he or she has noticed (that sound X is replaced by sound Y in context Z) and then treat the 'deviant' sound as though it were in fact an instance of the 'basic' sound. That is, in our example above the linguist could write *m* not only in words like *me* but also in those like *emphatic* as though they were pronounced in the same way because the difference in pronunciation is covered by the rule just formulated. This process of collapsing objectively different sounds into a single analytic unit makes life much easier for the linguist, but it also leads to important discoveries about sound systems at more abstract levels of analysis.

Now we come to the Zulu data. The relevant pair of sounds (see table 10) consists of two *o*-like sounds. We can distinguish them in the phonetic notation by using a capital *O* for one and a small *o* for the other. (This isn't a standard phonetic notation, but that needn't worry us here; it may have the advantage of being slightly easier for you to remember when I have explained the difference between the two sounds to you.) Neither of these sounds is particularly difficult to make, and you probably have similar sounds in your speech, but it is hard for me to describe the sounds to you by referring to words in your pronunciation of English because I don't know what your pronunciation is like. In my pronunciation the *o*-sound is somewhat like the vowel in *boat* and the *O*-sound like that in *ought*, but you may pronounce these English words quite differently from me, in which case the description I have just given will be misleading for you. If you know some French, then I can identify the *o*-sound with that in *chaud*, and the *O*-sound with the one in *bonne*. However, the most helpful description of the vowels will turn out to be a phonetic one, referring to the position of the tongue. You will find the following information essential for reaching a satisfactory solution to the Zulu problem.

The relevant part of your tongue is whichever part of it is closest to the roof of your mouth; we can call this the 'vowel-maker' (again, not a standard term). The vowel-maker moves in two dimensions: up and down, so that the gap between it and the roof of your mouth gets wider or narrower; and from back to front, so that it is nearer to your teeth (the front of your mouth) or to your throat. Both of the Zulu sounds with which we are concerned are made with the vowel-maker near the back of the mouth, and the difference between them is that the O-sound has a bigger gap between the vowel-maker and the roof of the mouth than the o-sound does – hence the use of a bigger O for the former. Zulu has four other vowel sounds which occur in our list of words: *i, e, a* and *u*. A hint to help you solve the problem is that you should pay special attention to these other vowels, and because of this you should know how all the vowel sounds are related to each other on the two phonetic dimensions just described. The letters used in the transcription have much the same values as in French or Spanish, except that *u* represents the sound of French *tout*, not *tu*. Figure 3 will help you to see how they are related to each other: *i* and *u* are both made with a narrow gap between the vowel-maker and the roof of the mouth, and *e, o* and O have wider gaps, but *a* has the widest gap of all. The essential point for you to remember is that *o* involves a narrower gap than O and that *i* and *u* have the narrowest gaps of all.

We are now almost ready for the Zulu data, except for a

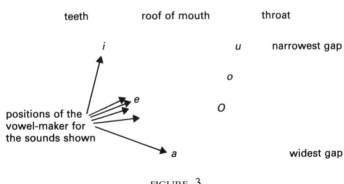

FIGURE 3

comment on the notation used for the consonants. Zulu is one of the languages which have 'click' sounds as consonants (which I mentioned briefly in chapter 5) – sounds like the one written as *tut-tut* in English or the one they use in Westerns when they want to get a horse to move. These are represented variously as *c*, *q* and *x* in the data. Another exotic sound is the one written as *B*, which is a *b* made by sucking in instead of blowing out. To be faithful to the facts of Zulu phonetics, we have to recognize these sounds, but you need assume that they are necessarily relevant to our problem.

Each of the Zulu words contains either *O* or *o*, along with other vowels, so the data are divided into two lists, according to which of these two vowels the words contain. Just to remind you what the problem is, you have to work out the relation between the *O*-sound and the *o*-sound in Zulu, and you start off with the information that they are examples of the phenomenon we discussed earlier in relation to the *m* in *emphatic:* one of them can be taken as a kind of distortion of the other, which has the effect of making the sound more similar to its phonetic context. This means that you have to do two things: you have to decide which of *o* and *O* is the 'normal' one and which the deviation, and you have to decide in which phonetic contexts the deviant one occurs. You should also be able to say in what particular respect the deviation makes *o/O* more similar to its context.

Table 10

words containing *O*		words containing *o*	
BOna	see	iBoni	grasshopper
BOpha	bind	umondli	guardian
mOsa	despoil	umosi	one who roasts
umOna	jealousy	inoni	fat
imOtO	car	udoli	doll
iqOlO	small of back	umxoxi	story-teller
ixOxO	frog	imomfu	jersey cow
isicOcO	head ring	lolu	this
ibOdwe	pot	isitofu	stove
isithOmbe	picture	nomuthi	and the tree
indOdana	son	udodile	you acted like a man
umfOkazi	strange man	ibokisi	box

Hints for working

Remember the three questions to be answered:

(1) What are the differences between the phonetic contexts in which O occurs and those in which *o* occurs?
(2) Which of O and *o* is the deviant one of the pair?
(3) Whichever of them is the deviant one, in what respects is this sound more similar to the contexts in which it occurs than the other one would have been in those contexts?

A quick glance through the words may already have given you the answer, in which case you may still find the following hints interesting, as they may tell you something about how your mind set about solving the problem. We can take the questions one at a time.

Basically, what you have to do is to find some pattern which occurs in the words in one of these columns but not in those in the other column. It is possible that the pattern you are looking for is a complicated one; for example, it could be that the essential difference between the first word in the O column (*BOna*) and the one in the *o* column (*iBoni*) is that the O occurs both after *B* and before *na*, whereas the *o* occurs between *iB* and *na*. However, you should always assume at first that the solution will be a simple one and accept a more complicated one only if it is forced on you by the data. You can take it for granted that problems set as exercises in analysis, such as this one, have been chosen precisely because they do allow simple solutions, so you ought to be able to reject out of hand the suggestion that the relevant contexts involve as much as two sounds on either side of the *o*/O vowel. What you are looking for, rather, is a context which consists of just one sound; and you should abandon this search only after you have exhausted all the possibilities. Furthermore, you should hope that the sound in question will be easy to define – that is, either it will be the same sound in each case or it will be one of a class of sounds which can be defined easily without just listing its members. You would also have to reject my earlier proposal on these grounds because you would have to say that *O* occurs either between *B* and *na*, or between *B* and *pha*, or . . . . In fact, your definition of the contexts would be more or less a copy of the list of words itself.

Another hint for finding the difference between the contexts of *O* and *o* is that you will probably make the best progress if you start by looking at the sounds immediately next to *o/O* to see if they constitute the relevant context and then, if that fails, start looking further afield, gradually considering more and more of each word.

Having worked out the differences between the contexts, you can tackle the other two questions. In order to decide which vowel is the deviant one, you need to decide which of them can best be explained as the result of a process of assimilation. You will find that there is one crucial set of words in the list: words in which the *o/O* vowel has no context at all, according to your definition of the relevant contexts. Whichever vowel occurs when there is no relevant context at all must obviously be the basic one because there is no context to cause it to deviate, so the other one must be the deviant one.

Finally, you have question 3: in what sense is the deviant member of the pair more similar to its context as a result of its deviation? To answer this, you must compare it with its context (as defined in your first two answers) and see if you can find any similarity between the two which is absent from the basic member and the contexts in which it occurs. You will find that the information that I gave earlier about phonetic relations among Zulu vowels is highly relevant here.

PROBLEM 3: BEJA RELATIVE CLAUSES

The next problem takes us into the syntax of Beja. What you need to do is to find an explanation for the fact that there are two ways of translating 'I saw a man whom I know' into Beja, which are different not only in the order of words but also in the ending that is added to one of the words. The Beja translations are these:

akteene tak rihan
tak akteeneeb rihan

As you can see, the words that change position between the two sentences are *tak* and *akteene(eb)*, and the word whose ending varies is the latter, which is *akteene* in one case and *akteeneeb* in the other. What you are looking for is a pair of closely related rules which will explain why *akteene tak* can be replaced by *tak akteeneeb* without any change of meaning.

Before I give you some more data, you may find it helpful to know a little more about how these words are pronounced. The consonants are pronounced in ways that seem natural to an English speaker, and the vowels are pronounced as in the Zulu exercise, except that a short *e* or *o* at the end of a word (like the *e* at the end of *akteene*) is pronounced as though it were a short *i*. That means that the short vowel at the end of *akteene* is pronounced in just the same way as the one at the end of *dabalo*, which I shall give in the data below, in spite of the difference in the spelling. Since I am the person responsible for this particular spelling, you might think I owed you an apology for making a bad job of it, but in fact it is useful to make this distinction in the spelling, because when the vowels are lengthened (shown by doubling) before the *b* ending, they turn into different long vowels, which are pronounced quite differently – a long *ee* sound in *akteeneeb* and a long *oo* sound in *dabaloob*. This will make your job a little easier, since you can now forget what I have just told you and analyse *akteene* and *dabalo* as though they did have different vowels at the end. I mention this point just to show you how a linguist can improve the analysis of one part of a language (in this case, the part that deals with the effect of adding a *b* and also a lot of other endings) by 'fiddling' slightly the analysis of another part.

Rather than give you a single list of sentences followed by hints on working, I shall give you the sentences a few at a time, so that you can concentrate on the many problems facing you one by one. Each of the following batches of sentences will throw a little extra light on the analysis of the two sentences we started with, which we can call the 'test sentences'. The first thing you need to do in analysing the test sentences is to work out what each of the three words *akteene(eb)*, *tak* and *rihan* means, given that the whole sentence means 'I saw a man whom I know'. One thing is clear: there are only three Beja words corresponding to seven English words, so we can't expect each Beja word to match an English word exactly. This is no surprise, given what we saw in chapter 5 about the capacity of Beja for putting a lot of information into a few words. The first two sentences should enable you to work out the meanings of the three Beja words.

| 1 | tak rihan | I saw a man |
| 2 | yaas rihan | I saw a dog |

(You may find it helpful to jot down the Beja words with their meanings on a separate bit of paper as you go through the data.) You probably needed no help in using sentences 1 and 2 to identify the meanings of *tak* and *rihan*, so the meaning of *akteen(eb)* must be just what is left over in the meaning of the test sentences.

We now extend the data by bringing in two extra words, *akra* and *dabalo*. You should decide what each of them must mean and how you think you might classify it in terms of a set of word classes like 'noun', 'adjective', 'verb' and so on.

| 3 | akra tak rihan | I saw a strong man |
| 4 | dabalo tak rihan | I saw a small man |

The meanings should be easy to identify. As for the word classes, it is fair to assume that if two words in different languages mean the same, then they belong to the same word class unless there is clear evidence to the contrary (as there may well be). You should apply the same procedure to identifying the word classes of *tak* and *rihan*, which will allow you to start formulating some general rules of Beja grammar to do with the order of words. Specifically, you should be able to formulate two rules of the form 'An X that belongs to a Y precedes/follows/precedes or follows the Y', where X and Y stand for the names of the word classes to which you have assigned *tak, rihan, akra* and *dabalo*. (Again it may be helpful to jot down your rules.)

Another order of words is possible in sentences with the meanings of 3 and 4. I repeat 3 and 4 here, with their alternative orderings as 3a and 4a:

3	akra tak rihan	I saw a strong man
3a	tak akraab rihan	I saw a strong man
4	dabalo tak rihan	I saw a small man
4a	tak dabaloob rihan	I saw a small man

Here you will notice that we have *akraab* instead of *akra* and *dabaloob* instead of *dabalo*. Since the meanings of the sentences are still the same, these differences in word form must leave the words' meanings unaffected, so (failing evidence to the contrary) you can assume that the word classes also stay the same. You should now be able to revise one of your earlier rules and formulate a third rule, relating to the form of some class of words and, in particular, to whether these words contain the ending *b*. (To help you I can tell you that you can ignore the changes in the length of the vowel before the *b* because there is a very general rule that lengthens vowels before a consonantal ending, so we can leave this general rule to take care of the vowel length.) We can now bring together the three rules that you have worked out:

Rule A   Any . . . . that belongs to a . . . . precedes/ follows it.

Rule B   Any . . . . that belongs to a . . . . precedes/ follows it.

Rule C   A   . . . . contains the suffix *b* if . . . .

By now you should know everything you need to know about *tak, rihan* and the *b* ending. We must turn to the word *akteene(eb)*, whose meaning you have worked out already. As we have seen, this word appears in two forms, with and without a *b* ending. You are now in a position to explain why this is, provided that you are willing to accept a particular classification of *akteene(eb)* in terms of the word classes used already. In other words, you can say to yourself: 'The rules I have already formulated will explain the alternation between *akteene* and *akteeneeb* provided that I classify the word as . . . . ; therefore it must be . . . . unless I can see a good reason for rejecting this analysis.' So your next job is to decide what word class *akteene(eb)* belongs to.

Having done this, you need to know how *akteene(eb)* is made up. You already know that the *b* is an ending which may or may not be present and that the second *e* before the *b* just marks the effects of the automatic vowel–lengthening rule, so we can now forget about the *eb* at the end and concentrate on *akteene*. You now need the following data:

5	tak akteen	I know a man
6	akteen	I know him

On the basis of this data, you should find it easy to find an ending in *akteene*, which leaves you with the job of deciding how this ending is used. The best way to set about this is to think of the ending as a device for changing the word class, so you need to compare the word class of *akteene* with that of what is left of the word when you remove the ending. You have already worked out the word class of *akteene*, so all you need to do is decide on the word class of the word which you get by removing the ending from *akteene,* which you should find easy. You can now complete the fourth rule:

Rule D   Adding the suffix . . . . to a . . . . changes it into a . . . .

You should now be wondering how general this rule is, so you can check it against the following sentences:

7	tak rihan	I saw a man
8	rihane tak akteen	I know a man whom I saw
9	tak rihaneeb akteen	I know a man whom I saw

I hope you found that all your rules were confirmed by these sentences. Assuming this to be the case, you have virtually finished the problem, and all you need to do is to go back to the test sentences and put into words why it is that both orders of *tak* and *akteene(eb)* are possible and why the *eb* is present in one case but not the other. Your explanation should be of the form: 'These alternatives are possible because *akteene(eb)* is a typical . . . ., and such variation is permitted for any . . . .; and it is a . . . . because it contains the ending . . . . added to . . . ., according to the general rule D.'

PROBLEM 4: ENGLISH TIME EXPRESSIONS WITH 'BEFORE'

For our last problem we turn from our 'exotic' languages to English, just to remind you that puzzles exist on your linguistic doorstep – as we have in fact already seen in our discussion of English in chapter 4. Since we have had one puzzle to do with pronunciation (Zulu) and one dealing with syntax and inflections (Beja), we had better take this problem from the other main area of language, meaning. We shall see how meaning can be out of step with syntax.

The problem involves the word *before*. *Before* may be followed by what traditional grammars call a clause – i.e. a sequence of words centring on a verb – but it may also be followed just by a noun:

> clause: He washed his hands before *he sat down*.
> noun: He washed his hands before *lunch*.

Now, if *before* is followed by a noun, the sentence may be ambiguous. An example of such a sentence is this: *He saw her before John*. According to one interpretation, this means 'He saw her before he saw John'; according to another, it means 'He saw her before John saw her'. Why is this sentence ambiguous, while the other one containing a noun (*He washed his hands before lunch*) only has one meaning? After a moment's thought you may regard this as a non-problem because the difference between the two sentences is obvious: *lunch* is the name of a time (short for *lunchtime*), whereas *John* is the name of a person. However, the question remains: why does this particular difference between *John* and *lunch* lead to ambiguity in one case but not in the other? In order to give a proper answer we shall have to explore the meaning of *before* a little.

What does a sentence like *He got up before 8.00* mean? The part of the meaning that we need to concentrate on is the part which deals with time (which we started to explore on pages 72–3, so my question could be rephrased as 'What does this sentence tell us about the time of getting up?' To make progress we shall have to introduce a small amount of notation, rather like the notation used in algebra. Let us represent the time of the event – in this case, his getting up – by E and let this stand for any time at all, as long as it is the same time whenever it is used in connection with a particular sentence. (This is the normal convention for algebra, whereby each letter is allowed to represent any number as long as it consistently stands for the same number on any given occasion when a formula is applied – e.g. in $a + b = ac$, the two *a*s must both stand for the same number, whatever this may be.)

We can now start analysing the meaning of *He got up before 8.00*, by breaking its meaning down into two bits, linked by virtue of the fact that they both contain a reference to our letter E. I shall provide the first bit, and your job is to give the second, which defines the relation between E and 8.00. Following the model of algebra, we can call these bits 'formulae' (though this isn't standard terminology in linguistics):

> sentence: He got up before 8.00.
> formula 1: He got up at E.
> formula 2: E . . . . 8.00.

In filling in your part of the second formula you will need to use a verb, and in English you can't use a verb without choosing between past tense and present tense. There is no need to worry about this choice, but the simplest thing is probably to use present tense verbs all the time.

Now try working out the two formulae for *He got up at 8.00*, to make sure you understand the system:

> sentence: He got up at 8.00.
> formula 1: . . . .
> formula 2: . . . .

Remember that both formulae must contain E.

We now have to make the analysis a little more complicated to allow for cases where we don't know precisely when the second time was, in contrast to the above sentences, where we knew that it was 8.00. It might be represented, for example, by the word *then*. We can call this second time the 'reference' time – the time to which we refer in identifying the time of the event. Just as we use E to stand for the time of the event, we can use R to stand for the reference time, whether or not we know exactly when R is. If you have to analyse the meaning of a sentence containing *then*, you can use R to stand for whatever time *then* refers to, so you ought to be able to complete the following analysis:

> sentence: He got up before then.
> formula 1: . . . .
> formula 2: E . . . . R

We can now go back to one of our original sentences, *He washed his hands before lunch*. If we assume in this case that R stands for the time of lunch, then you can easily work out the analysis:

> sentence: He washed his hands before lunch.
> formula 1: . . . .
> formula 2: . . . .

Furthermore, you can work out a general rule for the meaning of expressions introduced by *before* to cover those cases where *before* is followed by words that refer to a time (such as *lunch, then* or *8.00*):

Rule A   If a sentence contains *before* followed by an expression which refers to a time R, then its formula 1 contains E, and formula 2 is . . . .

The next thing for us to do is to consider the more complicated sentence with which we started, *He saw her before John*, which you will remember is ambiguous. The first thing that is clear is that Rule A does not apply at all to sentences like this, because *John* does not refer to a time. Since this is a perfectly good English sentence, we need another rule to cover it and similar sentences. To decide what this other rule should be, we must start with the other kind of construction introduced by *before* which I mentioned at the beginning of this discussion, namely constructions in which *before* introduces a clause (e.g. *He washed his hands before he sat down*). Here we shall need to provide an extra formula in the analysis, since we have an extra clause to analyse. We can call the two formulae for the clauses 1a and 1b, so that formula 2 is left for showing the time relations.

Now, how shall we analyse this sentence? You can probably already see the answer: we must let the formula for *he sat down* contain R, as the time at which he sat down, so that the clause introduced by *before* does exactly the same work as was done in the previous sentences by words like *8.00* and *lunch*. Thus, the second clause serves to identify the time R, and *before* tells us the relation between E and R as usual. You should be able to complete this analysis:

sentence: *He washed his hands before he sat down.*
formula 1a: He washed his hands at . . . .
formula 1b: He sat down at . . . .
formula 2:   E . . . . R

You can also work out the general rule to cover such cases:

Rule B   If a sentence contains *before* followed by a clause
           which refers to an event that happened at time R,
           then . . . .

With this analysis behind us, we can solve the problem of how to analyse *He saw her before John*. This means the same as either *He saw her before John saw her* or *He saw her before he saw John*, both of which are covered by the rule you have just formulated because in both cases *before* is followed by a clause. Since each of the two meanings of *He saw her before John* is the same as the meaning of one of these sentences, we can give it the same analysis; so for both meanings formula 1a will be the same ('He saw her at E'), and so will formula 2, but 1b will be 'He saw John at R' in one interpretation and 'John saw her at R' in the other. However, we still don't have a rule covering sentences like this because *before* is followed not by a clause but by a noun (*John*), so rule B doesn't apply to it. We need a third rule to tell us how to arrive at an analysis for a sentence in which *before* is not followed by a clause but is interpreted as though it were. The question is, where does the 'understood' clause come from? How is it that you had no difficulty in working out that one meaning of *He saw her before John* was the same as that of *He saw her before John saw her*? Why didn't you understand it to mean something like *He saw her before John kissed her*? I hope the answer is sufficiently obvious for you to complete the following rule:

Rule C   If a sentence contains *before* followed by an expression which is neither an expression of time nor a clause, then the sentence is interpreted as though *before* were followed by a clause; to work out what this 'understood' clause is, you . . . .

If you have filled in the blank part of this rule correctly, you will have provided an explanation for the ambiguity of *He saw her before John*. You should be able to develop an explanation along the lines of: 'This sentence is ambiguous because it is covered by rule C, which allows two interpretations because . . . .' In contrast, rule C does not apply to *He washed his hands before lunch*, which is covered by rule A, and since rule A is not formulated in such a way as to allow for ambiguities, we have an explanation for why this sentence only has one meaning. QED.

What I have tried to do in this chapter is to devise puzzles which are sufficiently precise to allow a simple solution but also sufficiently complex to require some thinking. I took you through the analysis in steps that were as small as I could manage in the hope that I would not lose you even if this kind of thinking doesn't come naturally; as I said earlier, I believe that many students simply lack experience and training and get much better with help. However, you may have found that I was giving you too much help and making you work too slowly; in that case, I hope you did some judicious skipping and took each exercise in the spirit in which I intended it. I can assure you that the exercises you might do on a course in linguistics would include some that would stretch you to your limits.

114

Puzzles

MY ANSWERS TO THE PROBLEMS

Problem 1: classical and vulgar Latin

Rule 1   Unstressed vowels in the last syllable but one are dropped.

Rule 2   Short *u* changes to *o*.

Rule 3   Long vowels become short.

Rule 4   Final *m* is dropped.

Rule 5   Short *i* changes to *e*.

Rule 6   If a word in classical Latin starts with two or more consonants, *e* is added before these consonants.

Problem 2: Zulu vowels

Question 1   The O vowel occurs when the next vowel is *a*, *e* or *O* or when there is no following vowel.

Question 2   The *o* vowel is the deviant one because O occurs where there is no following vowel and therefore no relevant context to cause deviation.

Question 3   The *o* vowel is made with a narrower gap than O, and the vowels which cause the deviation (*i*, *u*) are made with a narrower gap than the ones which don't cause it (*a*, *e*, O), so *o* is more similar to its context than O would be with respect to the size of the gap.

Problem 3: Beja relative clauses

Rule A   A noun that belongs to a verb precedes the verb.

Rule B   An adjective that belongs to a noun precedes or follows the noun.

Rule C   An adjective contains the suffix *b* if it follows its noun.

Rule D   Adding the suffix *e* to a verb changes it into an adjective.

The alternatives are possible because *akteene(eb)* is a typical adjective, and such variation is permitted for any adjective;

115

and it is an adjective because it contains the ending *e* added to a verb, according to the general rule D.

Problem 4: English time expressions with 'before'

He got up before 8.00.   E precedes 8.00.

He got up at 8.00.   He got up at E. E is 8.00.

He got up before then.   He got up at E. E precedes R.

He washed his hands before lunch.   He washed his hands at E. E precedes R.

Rule A   If a sentence containes *before* followed by an expression which refers to a time R, then its formula 1 contains E; formula 2 is 'E precedes R'.

He washed his hands before he sat down.   (1a) He washed his hands at E: (1b) He sat down at R; (2) E precedes R.

Rule B   If a sentence contains *before* followed by a clause which refers to an event that happened at time R, then E precedes R.

Rule C   If a sentence contains *before* followed by an expression which is neither an expression of time nor a clause, then the sentence is interpreted as though *before* were followed by a clause; to work out what this 'understood' clause is, you take the rest of the sentence and substitute the expression following *before* for any part of the sentence, provided the result makes sense.

The sentence is ambiguous because it is covered by rule C, which allows two interpretations because either *he* or *her* in *he saw her* could be replaced by *John*.

7

Theories: Boon or Bore?

Some people love theories; others distrust them intensely. The lovers think that theorizing is the highest form of intellectual activity because that is when you get nearest to reality, having fought clear of all the details and distractions of particular cases. The distrusters think that theories are distortions of reality, since reality is in fact the sum total of particular cases, and they see theories as a concession to our human frailty, which we need because our minds just aren't up to the job of understanding this reality directly. So the best we can do is to build ourselves an artificial world in our minds, populated with theories and idealizations. Then when we try to understand something in the real world, we shift the problem into the relevant part of our imaginary world and solve it there in the hope that the solution will apply equally to the real world. Theory lovers would disagree with the distrusters and would argue that you can't even identify a problem in the real world, let alone solve it, unless you've got some theories.

The point of saying all this is simply to draw your attention to the issue in case you hadn't already noticed it for yourself. Of course, what I said in the first paragraph is itself a theory – a testable generalization – which may or may not be right. One respect in which it certainly is not right is that many people don't fall neatly into one or the other of my two groups. Nevertheless, I think it is a fact of life that people have different attitudes to things that are labelled 'theories', and some feel much more positively towards them than others do. To some extent these differences seem to be a matter of upbringing – for example, the British as a whole have a reputation for distrusting theories, in contrast to the French – and students who approach linguistics from the side of the humanities will probably have had less positive experience of theorizing than those who come from the natural sciences.

Since linguists are like other people in this respect and are united only in their enthusiasm for studying language, we find similar differences among linguists in their attitudes to theories. Some linguists regard theorizing as their most valued activity and would in fact describe themselves as 'theoretical linguists'; others are proud of having their feet firmly on the ground and want more than anything else to produce reliable descriptions of particular languages. They would prefer to describe themselves as 'descriptive linguists'. And, of course, many others hover uncertainly between the two extremes. (My own position is near to the theoretical end of the spectrum, but I have a high regard for the work done by my colleagues at the descriptive end, so I prefer to think that linguistics is all the better for being practised by both types of linguist.)

Any course on linguistics will present you with some combination of the descriptive and the theoretical approaches, with more theory in some courses and less in others. However, every course contains some proportion of theory, and most courses contain a lot of it, so I want to spend this chapter telling you something about the theories that linguists have to offer.

HOW SOUNDS CHANGE

One of the first theories that achieved prominence in the world of linguistics was to do with the ways in which sounds change through time and was formulated by a group of young linguists in Germany just over a hundred years ago. Linguists had been aware for some time that the pro-nunciations of the words in a language could vary from one period to another, so that a word which occurred in (say) Shakespeare's English and still occurs in modern English might nevertheless have a different pronunciation now. To take an obvious example, Londoners in Shakespeare's time pronounced the *r* in words like *farm* but don't pronounce it nowadays. (The fact that the *r* is still pronounced in many parts of the English-speaking world doesn't affect the issue but just goes to show how unclear the notion 'English' is. The fact is that the pronunciation of words like *farm* changed over the years. If you are uncertain whether you pronounce the *r* in *farm*, see if you make it rhyme with *balm* or *calm*.) Our spelling of English gives us a good deal of information about the pronunication of much earlier times, and the *r* in our spelling of *farm* is just one example of many (others are the *k* of *knee*, the *gh* of *night*, and the different spellings of *meat* and *meet*).

The question is, how regularly do these changes apply? What the young German linguists did was to stand back from the mass of data which had accumulated by the end of the nineteenth century and try to make the simplest possible statement about it which was compatible with the facts (as they saw the facts). Their theory was that all sound changes apply in a completely regular way, in the sense that a particular change affects every single word which contains the sound in question (and, of course, in the context in question). So the loss of *r* in English words should, according to this theory, apply equally to every word in which *r* is in an 'exposed' position, as it is in *farm*. (You might try to work out just what positions would count as exposed in this sense, bearing in mind that the *r* was lost in *far* but not in *red* or *very*.)

By now you probably want to know whether this theory turned out to be right. One of the attractions of a theory like this one is that it makes such a sweeping claim that it ought to be easy to disprove if it's wrong; so all we need to overturn this theory is one example of one word, in one language, which has failed to be affected by one rule which should have applied to it. If we take the example I used, the loss of *r*, we need to look at the varieties of English which have been affected by it and find just one word which has resisted and has kept its *r*. Common sense tells us that language is a human institution, and human institutions are generally fairly wilful, so we should expect to find the odd exception to any rule. If you are a native speaker of English and you have no *r* in *farm*, you can test the theory for yourself. I think you will find that common sense is wrong in this case and that you have no exceptions. Assuming that this is so, we seem to have some very weak support for the theory that all sound changes are completely regular: we have looked at the effects of one sound change and found that it was completely regular. So far so good, but of course that in itself proves nothing because we still don't know whether the same will be true of other sound changes.

Unfortunately, it's not quite as easy as that to test this theory because there are a number of ways in which apparent counter-examples can be explained away. For example, a particular sound change applies only at a particular point in history, then finishes: the loss of *r* happened some centuries ago, and we no longer need to think of it as an active influence on the pronunciation of people like me (who have no *r* in *farm*) because all those *r*s are no longer there (except in the spelling), so they couldn't be affected by the sound change. But new words are being added all the time, so a new word could reintroduce a sound which had been affected by an earlier change and not be affected by that change simply because it is no longer active. An example of this situation is the word *Tass* (the name of the Soviet news agency), which is always pronounced with a short *a* (so far as I know), even though the southern British standard pronunciation for other words ending in *-ass* was affected some time ago by a change which lengthened the *a* (giving the long vowel of *grass, pass* and so on). So for every other apparant counter-example to the *a*-lengthening we must ask whether the word in question was around at the time when the change was active, and only when we have persuaded the rest of the world that the word was accessible to the change can we sit back and feel we have definitely found a counter-example to the theory.

Somewhat disappointingly, a century of very hard work and hard arguing still hasn't settled the issue, but it has been very productive in other ways, and it would be fair to judge the success of the theory against the positive effects that it has had. For one thing, it stimulated a great deal of excellent work on dialects, which was inspired largely by the desire to disprove the theory by showing that some changes which had produced dialect differences had applied irregularly. For another, it raised the quality of work dealing with the historical relations among ancient languages and their more recent 'offspring' (e.g. Latin in relation to the modern 'Romance' languages French, Italian, Spanish, Romanian and a few others). Take the case of two modern languages that we know: we want to find out for sure whether they are both descended from a common 'parent' language because the latter (if it ever existed) is no longer available through written records. We can answer the question by deciding whether or not pairs of words in the two languages are descended from a common parent word, and the standard method for doing so rests firmly on the assumption that sound changes are regular. Both of these developments are healthy (and have in turn led to other positive developments) and show how a theory which is clear and general can do good irrespective of whether it is true or not.

So now we come back to you and your attitude to theories. Let us suppose that you don't much like theories in general but that you have been willing to take my word about the benefits of this particular theory for the well-being of linguistics as a discipline. Most probably you have been saying to yourself, 'OK, so it's good for linguistics, but it leaves me absolutely cold.' I shall now try to persuade you that the theory of regular sound change might even have some interest for you as an individual.

First, you can be sure that you yourself are actively helping to propagate a handful of sound changes in your own speech. This must be so because languages are constantly changing in pronunciation matters (as in other areas, such as syntax), so at any moment various changes must be under way. Not that it is easy to identify the currently active changes because of the great variety of speech that exists at any given moment in any community, but there are techniques available which linguists can apply and which allow them to be fairly sure about which sounds are changing. (For example, it is becoming increasingly common in England for a glottal stop to be used instead of a *t* at the end of a word, especially if the next word begins with a consonant.) After a certain amount of training in these techniques, combined with some information from books, you could identify some of the changes which your own speech reflects, and then you could apply the theory of regular sound change to these changes and ask whether they are regular. In other words, you could ask whether your own behaviour is regular, as predicted by the theory. Whichever way the answer goes, it is sure to be of interest to you.

Another way in which the theory may be relevant to your interests is through its relation to etymology, which many students find fascinating. We have already seen that historical linguists use the theory of regular sound change as a criterion for testing the connections between words in different languages: if the two words have a common ancestor, then it ought to be possible to trace them both back to this common ancestor, and any differences in form between either word and the ancestor should be explicable in terms of regular sound changes. The term that linguists use for describing pairs of words that are related in this way is 'cognate' – so, for example, the English word *four* and the German word *vier* (which means 'four') are said to be cognates.

The theory of regular sound change can make the study of etymology much more interesting because one pair of cognates can lead to another. Let us suppose that you know that the German word *Zoll* (pronounced *tsol*), meaning 'customs', is a cognate of the English *toll*. You can assume that whatever sound change led to the difference in their pronunciation was regular, so you can expect other English words beginning with *t* to have a cognate in German that begins with *z*, pronounced *ts*. If you know some German, think of as many German words as you can that begin with *z*, and check each one for a cognate in English; and you can extend the search to words with *z* in other positions, just in case the sound change affected these. After this hunt you might have arrived at the following list:

ENGLISH	GERMAN
two	zwei ('two')
ten	zehn ('ten')
to, too	zu ('to, too')
wart	Warze ('wart')
plant	Pflanze ('plant')

The nice thing about this list, from your point of view, is that you have actually discovered it for yourself.

You could try a similar exercise in relation to French or Spanish, though the connections between these languages and English are much more remote than the one between English and German (which are separated by only a couple of thousand years of history). For example, you could look for the cognates of *foot, tooth, two* and *ten*, and try to work out a general rule connecting the pairs.

Occasionally you will find that words which look at first sight as though they must be cognates turn out not to be – for example, English *have* looks similar to French *avoir*, doesn't it? But the historical linguists tell us that *avoir* is descended from Latin *habere* and that the cognate in Latin of English *have* is not *habere* (although this actually means 'have') but rather *capere*, which means 'take'. So you can see that the theory of regular sound change makes etymology into something like a science and lifts it well above the level of common sense and speculation.

HOW GENERAL IS GENERAL?

We have assumed a very simple definition of 'theory' so far: a theory is a testable generalization. We have discussed one example which would count as a theory by anyone's definition, the theory that all sound changes are regular, but theories in fact come in all shapes and sizes, and there is no reason to assume that theories must be as general as this one. Indeed, there is nothing to stop a theory from being very specific indeed – for example, one of the exercises in chapter 4 asked you to consider the first sound in the word *university* and to determine whether it is a vowel or a consonant. Say you answered, 'It is a consonant', this could count as a theory about the pronunciation of the word *university*, to the effect that whenever the word *university* is pronounced it starts with a consonant. So in this respect you were making (or at least implying) a generalization, and this generalization is testable because we have a criterion for deciding whether a sound is a consonant or a vowel when used in an English word, namely how it affects the choice between *a* and *an* (do we say *a university* or *an university*?). However, when we were talking at the start of this chapter about attitudes to theories, we had in mind not this kind of 'theory' but rather much broader generalizations comparable with the one about the regularity of sound changes. There doesn't, however, seem to be any obvious cut-off point at which we could say, 'Anything below this level of generality is too specific to count as a theory', so I shan't try to make any such distinction.

Indeed, I could use this fact as an argument to persuade you to take a more positive view of theories: after all, what you think of as a theory is just the same kind of thing as the more specific facts and claims that you count as the ground that you like to keep your intellectual feet firmly on. Thus I could take you off in various directions towards more general claims, starting with the very specific claim that *a* is used before a consonant and *an* before a vowel, and there would be no clear point at which you would be entitled to shout, 'Stop! I'm happy with facts, but I'll have nothing of your theories!'

For example, we could consider the implications for the language of those speakers who have no *h*-sound in their pronunciation of words like *house*. We might wonder whether the rules for such speakers are to all intents and purposes the same as for people who pronounce the *h*-sound, except that at the last moment, when they are poised to produce the *h*, so to speak, they decide to leave it out (through idleness, for example). This would be one theory; an alternative would be that such speakers simply have no *h* in *house*, just as other speakers have none in *honest, hour* or *owl*. So the question of their deciding not to pronounce it does not arise because there is no reason why they should pronounce it. If the first theory is right, then such speakers should select *a* before *house* because they have a consonant (*h*) at the start of this word; if the second theory is the correct one, they should use *an* because *house* begins with a vowel. So here we are faced by a question of fact for deciding between two rival theories: do people who 'drop' the *h* of *house* use *a* or *an*? If you are used to hearing such people, then you will probably have no difficulty in answering this question and in deciding in favour of the second theory. Having taken this step, you could then go on to develop more general theories about the relations among alternative pronunciations and their users.

Another direction in which the 'theory' about the choice between *a* and *an* could take us would be towards a much more general theory about words and their boundaries. In choosing between *a* and *an*, all we need to know about the next word is the nature of the first sound (consonant or vowel?); there are (virtually) no exceptional words which take the 'wrong' form of *a(n)* as far as this rule is concerned. (The 'virtually' is there because there are some people who use *an* before *hotel* even when they pronounce the *h*; I propose to cheat and forget about this awkward fact for the time being.) Do any other words behave like *a(n)*, with two forms that are chosen according to the pronunciation of the start of the next word? Yes: exactly the same is true of *the*, which has two pronunciations, one like the sound at the end of *opera* and the other like the vowel in *me*, chosen again according to whether the next word starts with a consonant or a vowel. Are *a(n)* and *the* part of a more general pattern, involving other words ending in the same sounds? No. No other word that ends in the vowel *a* has another form with *an*, nor does any have the alternation shown by *the*. So how about this theory: any word which is like these two in having an irregular change in its own form must be sensitive to a very simple, regular difference in its context, such as that between consonants and vowels at the start of the next word? Or, better still, an even more general theory: no rule may tolerate irregularity in more than one place?

By this point in the string of theories-built-on-theories you may well have begun to feel decidedly queasy; you may even have thrown the book down in disgust. This would be quite a healthy reaction to the last two theories, which weren't meant to be taken too seriously. (They *may* be true, but I've got so little evidence to support them that they're no more than guesses, alias hypotheses.) On the other hand, I hope you can see how one theory can lead to another more general one as a possibility to be tested, and this is how we make progress in really understanding our subject-matter, as opposed to simply enlarging, correcting and cataloguing it. The problem is that there is an inverse relation between value and reliability in the world of theories: the more general a theory is, the more it helps us to understand but the harder it is to be sure that it is right. A theory like the one about the choice between *a* and *an* is comfortably solid (though even here we might have qualms about the word *hotel*) but it doesn't explain anything beyond the behaviour of this one pair of word-forms. At the other extreme the theory about rules never tolerating irregularity in more than one place is beautifully general, and to the extent that it is true it could explain a lot of things about a lot of rules – but alas, it may not be true, and it may be a long time before we shall know whether it is or not.

The theories that I have taken as examples have naturally been restricted to certain small areas of the field covered by linguistics – sound change and variation in word form. However, every area has its theories, and we could have taken examples from other areas like syntax, semantics, psycho-linguistics and so on. You will probably have noticed, in fact, that the kinds of things we have been talking about in this chapter have been very similar to things that have come up for discussion in previous chapters. This is natural, since any claim made by a linguist is a theory (given our definition), to the extent that it is general and testable, so we have really been talking about theories all along, though it is only in this chapter that we have focused on this fact.

THEORETICAL PACKAGES

If you were to ask some linguistics students what they understood by 'theory' in relation to linguistics, they would probably tell you about something which I prefer to call a 'theoretical package' because it is just that – a collection of separate theories which are presented as a single package. (A typical package might include theories about phonology, grammar and semantics, plus various other theories about matters such as how we learn language as children.) Teaching is often built around these pacakges, and it might take as many as twenty hours of lectures just to introduce the main features of a single one. This gives an idea of their complexity and richness.

Linguists have been constructing these packages since at least the start of the twentieth century, so by the 1980s we have an impressively long list of packages to our credit (or discredit, according to how you see this proliferation of alternatives). Each one has a name (which is generally written with capital letters, for no very good reason), though the names are often not particularly illuminating for the uniniti-ated: Glossematics, Tagmemics, Systemic Grammar, Strati-ficational Theory, Prosodic Analysis, Case Theory, Trace Theory, Relational Grammar, Transformational Generative Grammar, Generative Phonology, Upside-down Phonology, Natural Generative Phonology, Functional Grammar, Mon-tague Grammar and so on. This list is by no means complete, so it is easy to see that no student will have time to become familiar with all of them, however enthusiastic he or she feels about theoretical packages. What generally happens is that one (or perhaps two) of these packages is presented in some detail, and then passing references may be made to other packages. It's unlikely, then, that you'll be in a position, at the end of a course in linguistics, to assess the relative pros and cons of all the packages which are available. Indeed, it is unlikely that anyone will ever be in a position to do so, given the amount both of time and of sympathy that is needed to become sufficiently familiar with a package to assess it reliably.

You may wonder why linguists present their theories in labelled packages, especially when there are so many packages to choose from. Is it because the theories in each package are so inextricably bound up with one another that you can't accept one without accepting the lot? Some linguists would claim that this is so, and there is certainly some truth in it. Some of the main differences do in fact stem from differences in the assumptions on which the theories in the packages are based, so if you change the assumptions, the effect is to abandon the whole of the package. However, this is by no means the whole story because very few assumptions or theories are completely unique to any one package, and the ways in which they are combined often seems fairly random.

Another reason why linguistic ideas are divided into packages is a social one, to do with the ways in which linguists, like most academics, like to belong to groups of like-minded scholars, identifiable by a labelled package of beliefs. There are many reasons for this tendency, some good, some not so good. Belonging to a community reduces the risk that your good ideas will die with you because by the time you die (or retire) they may have been adopted by the next generation members of the community. It also provides a supply of people with whom you can discuss ideas with a good chance of being understood. These are just two of the good reasons for academic groupings, but there are less good reasons as well, such as the fact that if you can identify yourself as a member of group X, then you will share in the glory of group X (if it has any glory); and if you can convince yourself that only the members of group X have a satisfactory approach to your subject, then there will be no need to try to read books and papers written by non-members because there is no chance that they will have anything useful to say. I think most of our students develop a fairly healthy scepticism about the academic world during their course in linguistics, and this is probably a valuable part of their education.

If what I have just said makes me appear cynical about theoretical packages in linguistics, I should restore the balance by saying that I myself have been responsible for somewhat more than my fair share of these labelled packages, and I think it is important for linguists to go on developing (and abandoning) packages, as long as they can avoid the negative effects that I have just referred to. If part of the need for packaging our theories is a social one, then so be it – we linguists are, after all, people, and we belong to a society which is going to be responsible for the perpetuation of any good ideas we may have. In any case, theoretical packages are a fact of life.

They have one advantage for students, as a matter of fact, in that students can explore a particular package without finding too many inconsistencies. The most widely known and taught package is the one called Transformational Generative Grammar (invented by Noam Chomsky, the most famous modern linguist), and it is almost certain that any course in linguistics will include a serious study of this package. This means that you would learn about the initial assumptions of the package and would then be taken through the various consequences of these assumptions as they are applied to language data; and if the teaching was done well, you would probably enjoy the experience of gradually coming to terms with a complex but coherent system of theories. Moreover, since the package is not only well known but also fairly clearly defined, it has been possible for some very talented teachers to produce first-rate textbooks to help you through this particular maze, whereas if the theories had not been packaged in this way, it would have been much harder to anticipate the particular combinations of theories that students would want or need to know about. As it happens, I think this particular package is wrong in some quite fundamental ways, but I still think it is a healthy experience for students to work their way through it.

In this chapter I have tried to make three points:

(1) that linguists, like other people, differ in their attitudes to general theories, ranging from the most 'theoretical' to the most 'descriptive', and that this variety is likely to be reflected in any course on linguistics;

(2) that general theories need not frighten you, since they are not very different from more specific 'facts', and you may become quite fond of them, with familiarity;

(3) that linguists tend to present their wares in 'packages' of theories which can be considered on their individual

merits to a much greater extent than is sometimes
implied, but that you will certainly become very much
aware of the existence of at least one of these packages
during a course in linguistics, and to some extent you
may be glad of this, as it will make your life easier.

8

The Great Issues (Grey Tissues?)

The 'great issues' of linguistics are the talking points that tend to fire people's imaginations and that strike them as rather more important in an absolute sense than some of the more technical points that arise, however interesting the latter may be. We have already aired a couple of them, in chapter 2: are technologically more advanced societies associated with more advanced languages? And do we follow our linguistic models in a slavish fashion, or in a way that shows the exercise of free will? You probably felt that the discussion of these issues was too limited when you read chapter 2; if so, I am fully satisfied – after all, my purpose is to persuade you to investigate linguistics more fully, rather than to try to give you a potted version of the findings of linguistics in this little book. In any case, the answers to all the important questions are complicated, and in most instances they are highly controversial, so each question deserves a whole book to itself. At the risk of increasing your frustration, I shall adopt the same policy in the present chapter: I shall raise the questions and outline some of the things that a linguist can say about them, but definitive answers will be few and far between. Here is a list of the issues I shall raise:

(1) How efficient is language?
(2) Is translation possible?
(3) Could there be a world language?
(4) Can we think without language?
(5) Does language influence thought?

(6) Is language different from everything else?
(7) Can other animals speak?
(8) Are there racial differences in language?
(9) Are we born to speak?
(10) How old is language?

If some of these issues interest you more than others, please feel free to skip; but you may find that the interconnections between the issues make it advisable to read through from the beginning.

HOW EFFICIENT IS LANGUAGE?

Some people complain about the difficulty of putting their thoughts into words and see language as a rather inefficient and clumsy tool which requires great skill on the part of its users. Such people are typically poets, who sweat blood over the wording of a single sentence, but you may have experienced similar frustrations at times, when trying to write an essay, for example, or to express your feelings on some complex subject. There are other people, though, whose view of language is much more positive. Not surprisingly, you may feel, linguists tend to belong to this group and to be overwhelmed by the subtlety and complexity of language. It is a widespread view among linguists that every language is perfectly adapted to the needs of the community that uses it, which means that language, in its various manifestations through individual languages, must be perfectly efficient. After you have followed a linguistics course for a while, you might well come to share this opinion, though your conclusions would probably be based on a rather small amount of data (a small part of the structure of just one or two languages). Is it possible to reconcile these views? And if not, who is right?

As so often turns out to be the case, at least part of the disagreement comes from the fact that the two groups are talking about different things. The complainers are talking about the difficulty of sorting out one's ideas to put them into a form which is suitable for coding into language, whereas the praisers are taking this operation for granted and saying that any suitably sorted message can be coded into the language of the person concerned. And once we have put the praisers' position like this, of course, it doesn't seem to amount to much of a case because it consists of nothing more than the claim that anything which is codable is codable. Nevertheless, we can still ask how far the difficulties of sorting out one's ideas are due to the clumsiness of language and how far they are related to the matter of skill in sorting out ideas.

Take a simple example. Suppose you wanted to tell someone else about the overall structure of this book, how would you put this information into words? (The relevant fact is that I have divided the book into nine chapters.) You have two problems in deciding how to translate your knowledge into a sentence. The first is that a sentence consists of words, and words express complex bundles of meaning which may offer you a number of alternative ways of packaging the message you want to convey. For instance, you can express the part:whole relation between the book and its chapters by means of a number of different expressions, each of which presents it in a different way: *contains, consists of, comprises, has . . . in it, falls into, is divided into, has, there are . . . in . . .* and so on. So the first problem is choosing among this range of options. The second problem is closely related, namely that you have to decide how best to present the information from the point of view of the listener, which means (among other things) deciding what the listener already knows. For example, you may or may not have already talked about the book, so you have to choose between *a book I'm reading at the moment, the book, it* and so on. Again you have to choose, which is a problem. Moreover, you have to decide in which order to present the elements (the book and the chapters) according to which will make it easier for the listener, and here you come back to the choice among expressions for the part:whole relation, because you have the following options (among others). I shall assume that you have chosen to use *the book*:

The book contains nine chapters.

There are nine chapters in the book.
Nine chapters are contained in the book.
Nine chapters make up the book.

The point of the example is that there are very many ways of expressing the same idea, and you have to work out which is best for your particular purposes. You have to take account of a lot of different factors, including others which I haven't mentioned here, such as style: *comprise*, for example, is relatively high-flown and not suitable when talking to a friend. And if such problems arise when you have a relatively simple idea to express, you can expect trouble when the ideas get more complex.

Returning to the efficiency of language, you can see the above discussion in either of two ways: either you can blame language for offering too many options and decide that language would be more efficient if it offered just one way of expressing a given idea (e.g. just one expression for describing part:whole relations), or you can praise language for offering such a wealth of alternatives, each appropriate for a different nuance of communicative need – in which case, of course, you have to show that each of the alternatives is more appropriate for a different set of circumstances than all the other expressions. We have now reached the point where it is possible to define a research programme which might settle the issue: we need to take some range of alternatives, such as the one discussed above, and work out exactly what differences there are among the alternatives. If there are few or none, the blamers are right and language over-provides; if all, or nearly all, the alternatives are suitable for different occasions, then the praisers win. Unfortunately, this research waits to be done.

There is another question we can ask, however, which is easier to answer. Are there any cases in which a language can be shown to under-provide? To answer this we need to find gaps in the patterns that are allowed by our own language, English, and that cause communication problems of which we can be aware. I think the evidence here is clear: there are such gaps, though you may never have noticed them because they raise problems so rarely. One example is the lack of a word meaning 'brother or sister' (comparable with the specialized word 'sibling' used by anthropologists or the German word *Geschwister*). Because of this you can say 'Have you any children?' or 'Have you any parents?' but not 'Have you any . . . ?', where the blank would be filled by a word meaning 'brother or sister'. Another example, of which you may be more aware, is the lack of a neutral term for addressing an adult whose name you don't know, especially a male (compare the very useful French *Monsieur*). *Sir* implies subservience; *you* (as in *Hey, you*!) is rude; *mister* and *mate* are non-standard; and simple *excuse me* may not be appropriate (e.g. if the person needs to be warned about an immediate danger). Shifting to syntax, what is the sentence you would use if you wanted to refer to two sets of neighbours, instead of the straightforward question *How big a house do your neighbours have?*.

If these examples have persuaded you that English makes some ideas relatively hard to express, simply because of the gaps in its expressive resources, then you will have to agree that at least one language (English) is not perfectly suited to the needs of its users. How we generalize to other languages and how we decide on the exact balance between efficiency and inefficiency for each language are major research questions.

IS TRANSLATION POSSIBLE?

This question is closely related to the first one because you can take it as a question about the relations between gaps in different languages. Do all languages have the same gaps? If not, then in a sense translation between languages is likely to be to that extent imperfect. As a matter of fact, we have already answered this question because I pointed out that German has a word for the concept 'brother or sister' which constitutes a gap in English. This means that some German sentences will be hard, or even impossible, to translate satisfactorily into English. Take the German sentence *Ich kenne seine Brüder*; this translates easily and satisfactorily into *I know his brothers*. Now replace *Brüder*, 'brothers', by *Geschwister*, 'brothers and/or sisters', which gives no indication of the sex of the people referred to. How do we translate *Ich kenne seine Geschwister*? *I know his brothers* clearly won't do, nor will *I know his sisters*. Even *I know his brothers and sisters* gives too much information because he may have no sisters (or no brothers), as far as the German sentence is concerned. This leaves *I know his brothers or his sisters*, but this is a very odd sentence because it implies that the speaker doesn't know which he knows. It is hard to think of any satisfactory translation for the German sentence, even if we abandon the aim of translating each German word by a single English one.

You may feel that examples like this aren't too important because of the relative rarity of gaps of which we are aware. However, there is a more serious problem. Take two languages associated with very different cultures. Each may be quite adequate to the needs of its own culture but not to those of the other culture. So when some item of culture is referred to in its 'own' language, it may be very difficult (or impossible) to translate the sentence concerned into the other language. We can see such differences even between French and British culture. For example, French people don't play cricket, but (some) British people do, so English has a rich vocabulary for things to do with cricket, while French has none at all. This being so, I assume there will be no satisfactory translation for a sentence like *The batsman drove past silly-mid-on*.

So far the answer seems to be that translation between languages isn't always possible. However, we can now complicate the picture by taking a more realistic view of the notion 'language' and see that at least some of the translation problems that we have just considered are very similar to problems that arise in communication between people who speak the same language. Take the last example, about cricket. The fact is that Americans don't play cricket either, so the sentence about driving past silly mid-on would be just as incomprehensible to an American speaker of English as it would be to a Frenchman if we left the English words, as

English words, in the middle of a French sentence (something like *Le batsman a drivé au delà du silly mid-on*). So the problem arises not from the difference between English and French as such but from the difference between English-for-cricketers and French-for-non-cricketers. Moreover, it is quite likely that there is some small community somewhere that speaks French and plays cricket and (presumably) has a full range of terminology for cricket. This points up the fact that different speakers of the same language have more or less different versions of it – in this case, English may or may not contain cricketing terminology.

But such differences need not apply between large communities, such as the British and American communities; they may be found within communities and can be distributed in very complex ways among individual members. For example, it is quite possible to know the term *batsman* but not *silly mid-on* (though probably not vice versa), and a person in that state of semi-ignorance would still have some problems in understanding our sentence, though not as many as an American. Similarly, linguistics students typically know some of the technical terminology of linguistics, but not all of it, so they are typically baffled some of the time in lectures.

The real issue, then, is whether communication is possible via language, and the problems of translation are just a special case. This brings us back to the first question, about the efficiency of language, because we need to know how communication takes place via language before we can evaluate the success of the contribution that language makes. It is often assumed that all the information conveyed by a sentence is expressed directly and literally by the words in the sentence, but this is not so. Rather, the information depends on the words in combination with the context and the general knowledge of the listener.

For example, take the sentence *The price was wrong*. First of all, imagine this in a statement like the following: *I wanted to buy the jacket, but the price was wrong.* Here the price is clearly the price of the jacket – but how do we know? There is nothing in the sentence itself to show it, but we all know that when we buy things we have to pay a price determined by the seller, so we put two and two together and make four. Moreover, we also know that what was wrong with the price was that it was too high. Once again, this is information which we add to what is literally conveyed by the words, and we add it by applying our general knowledge to the literal meaning of the words in the sentence.

In contrast, we add a very different interpretation to the same words in a different context: *I nearly sold the jacket, but when I was checking it, I found the price was wrong.* Here, all we know about the price is that it wasn't the right one, though we may infer from what we know about the ethics of trading that it was too low – that is, the opposite of the information we added in the first case.

What this all seems to mean is that the success of communication does not depend exclusively on the speaker and listener sharing exactly the same meanings for the words used, since the listener can often guess the intended meaning from the context with some degree of accuracy. Furthermore, if you hear a word you don't know at all, you don't just give up – you try to guess its meaning on the basis of the context. (This is probably the way in which you learned the meanings of most words when you were a child – very few words would have been explained to you explicitly). So maybe communication isn't as difficult as I was implying above, provided that the speaker and listener are prepared to put enough effort into it. And the same goes, presumably, for translation as a special case of bridging the communication gap.

COULD THERE BE A WORLD LANGUAGE?

Many people have been struck during the past century by the extent to which international conflicts are due to misunderstandings and the extent to which these misunderstandings are due to differences between the languages of different nations. We have just been considering some of the difficulties that can arise, and of course it is obvious that when you are stranded in a foreign country and know nothing of the language, your chances of successful communication are poor. It is natural, then, to ask whether it would be possible to introduce and disseminate a 'world language', which everyone in the world would learn and would thereby be enabled to communicate satisfactorily with everyone else in the world. Seen from the point of view of a linguist, how realistic is this idea?

There are two separate questions to be considered. The first is whether a suitable language could be found; and the second is whether the chosen language could be disseminated sufficiently widely. As for the selection of a language, there are two obvious objections to adopting an existing language: it would be unfair on all those people who had to learn it as a second language, in contrast to people who spoke it from childhood; and existing languages are more complicated and difficult to learn than they need be. For example, if English was chosen, you and I would be in a privileged position simply because of our ability to use it, and everyone else would have to put in a lot of effort simply learning all our irregular verbs and nouns, not to mention the often arbitrary details of syntax (e.g. we say *sufficiently big*, but not *enough big* – *enough*, unlike every other such word, follows the word to which it belongs).

In view of the difficulties of using an existing language, it might be better to sit down and create a new language, which would favour nobody because it would be nobody's native language and which would be easier to learn than an existing language. Such languages have been constructed, the most successful one being Esperanto, which is said to have been mastered by over 2 million people. Even these specially constructed languages are generally very heavily biased towards the languages of Western Europe, but no doubt linguists could help to reduce this bias, and a language could be produced which was roughly of equal difficulty for speakers of all languages. (Assuming between 4,000 and 5,000 languages in the world, each language might be allowed to contribute, say, two items of vocabulary and one rule of grammar.)

The second question is more tricky: assuming that a world

language had been chosen, how widely could it be disseminated? How could a sufficiently large number of people be motivated to learn it to make it worth other people's while also to learn it? Suppose you had been born into a world where everyone else spoke this language (even if only as a second language); it would clearly be not just advantageous but absolutely essential for you to learn it as well. But if only one other person, living on the other side of the globe, already spoke it, there wouldn't be much point in your learning it too on the off-chance that you might one day meet up with that person. How do you get from the latter state of affairs to the former? Presumably it all has to start with the kind of people who are likely to meet people from a wide range of other countries – diplomats, hitch-hiking students, soldiers and the like. Even if such people could be persuaded to learn the new language, there is no guarantee that it would be passed on to their fellow-countrymen with fewer international contacts – but maybe that wouldn't matter too much.

There are other factors to consider too before embarking on such an ambitious project – such as the very long-term question of how to prevent the language from fragmenting into dialects and (in due course) into languages. However, it is not obvious that a world language is out of the question, and the issues it might raise need to be considered seriously from the special perspective that linguistics can offer.

CAN WE THINK WITHOUT LANGUAGE?

We can start to answer this question with the observation that we sometimes think with language – for example, if you are given a bit of mental arithmetic, you will probably find yourself working through the problem in words, under your breath. So for some kinds of thinking, putting the problem into words is helpful or even essential. The question is whether we ever think without making some use of language to formulate our thoughts to ourselves. The fact that we don't always mutter to ourselves when we are thinking isn't conclusive, of course, because we could be using ordinary sentences, planned in the usual way but just not converted into actual sounds. For instance, you can run through the words of a poem to yourself, and you may be reading this book quietly to yourself, which is the passive equivalent of producing unpronounced words.

Although you're unlikely to find a clear and definitive answer to this question, there are a number of points that are probably fairly uncontroversial. One is that there are some concepts which you have only because you heard them talked about. An example of such a concept would be 'germ' – you almost certainly came across this concept first by meeting the word *germ* and trying to work out (or to find someone to explain to you) what it meant – in contrast to concepts like 'food' or 'bed', which you may well have arrived at long before you discovered that they had names. Typically, the further a concept is from your direct experience, the more likely it is that you will acquire it in the first place via language. Thus if we take the general question to be 'Could we think as we do now if we had no language?', then the answer is probably 'no' because at least some of the thoughts we have now involve concepts which we wouldn't have had if we didn't have language.

On the other hand, once we have acquired a concept there is no reason for thinking that we necessarily connect it, every time we think about it, with the word which originally led us to form the concept. After all, it is common experience that it is sometimes difficult to make precisely this connection when you are talking and are stuck for a word which is 'on the tip of your tongue'. Nor is it necessary to believe that we formulate all our thoughts in terms of suppressed sentences, as we saw when we discussed the efficiency of language. We saw there that when you are speaking (or writing) you have to sort out your thinking into a form which you can translate directly into a sentence; but this implies that your thinking is not in such a form until you make the effort necessary to shape it. If we were to maintain that all thinking is done in the form of suppressed sentences, there would be a danger of having to postulate an infinitely long string of planning steps because each sentence is the result of sorting out an earlier form of thinking into a codable form, so if the earlier form was itself a sentence, then that in turn must have been formed out of an earlier form and so on ad infinitum.

This is a complicated matter, and it may be that we should allow for 'sentences' which are more abstract than suppressed sentences consisting of particular words from a particular language, and that these more abstract 'sentences' are what thought consists of; in which case, of course, you will want to know what they have to do with ordinary language. You can probably imagine how the arguments and counter-arguments could mount up in an area like this – and they do.

DOES LANGUAGE INFLUENCE THOUGHT?

We have just seen that language does influence thought in at least one respect, namely that it leads us to acquire concepts which we wouldn't otherwise have (e.g. 'germ'). Moreover, I hope you agree with me that some of your thinking uses language as a tool, in the sense that you produce sentences to help you to think through a problem (e.g. mental arithmetic). In both cases we can say quite clearly that language influences thought, in that your thinking is different from what it would have been if you had lacked those particular bits of language.

At the same time we have seen that languages, and even individuals, can differ greatly in the concepts for which they have expressions (e.g. cricket terminology). If we put these two observations together, we come to the conlusion that people are likely to acquire different ranges of concepts according to the linguistic company that they keep. If you are surrounded by cricket-playing English speakers, you will learn the word *batsman* and probably also the concept 'batsman'; if not, not.

So far, so good – but hardly surprising. However, the differences between languages can be more subtle than simply a matter of having or not having expressions for a particular area of life. Two languages may both allow you to refer to

142

some area but may lead you to divide it up differently. For example, English and German treat the area of 'fungi' differently. In English we have the words *mushroom, toadstool mould* and *fungus*. Of these *fungus* is the most general and covers the other three, plus various other things (e.g. one can be inflicted with a skin disease caused by a fungus which is not a mould and certainly not a mushroom or a toadstool). The word *mushroom* is used to refer to one particular edible variety of fungus with a white outer surface and pink or brown inside. In German we find the word *Pilz* corresponding to *fungus* and the word *Champignon* (borrowed from French) for *mushroom* but nothing at all corresponding exactly to either *toadstool* or *mould*. For the latter there are two words (*Schimmel* and *Kahm*, according to whether the mould is growing on a dry surface or on a liquid), but for *toadstool* there is no word at all. This means that there is no need for a German speaker to have the concept 'toadstool', bringing together all fungi which are bigger than mould but excluding mushrooms, in contrast to an English speaker, who must have this concept if the word *toadstool* is to have any meaning at all. Of course, we should need to have some independent evidence for the lack of this concept in the mind of a German speaker, but cognitive psychologists have ways of investigating such things. If it did turn out that German speakers in general had no concept 'toadstool' (as seems quite likely), then this would be an example of two communities thinking differently because they speak different languages.

There has been a great deal of discussion about this possibility in relation to more general differences in thought patterns, such as the conception of time, and the most that can be said about the debate is that it is still going on after several decades. The implications are clear: if it turns out that important differences in thought patterns are indeed caused by the speaking of different languages, then this could go some way to explaining why communication between people from different nations (e.g. diplomats) is often so unsuccessful – they think differently, so how can their minds meet? If so, we should have another important argument in favour of a world language, since this would guarantee at least some similarity between the ways in which representatives of different nations thought.

At one level it is obvious that language is different from everything else: language, and only language, involves words, sentences and so on. The question is also a more subtle one: if we define language with reference to this difference (language is the knowledge and use of words), then do we find that it has any additional major differences compared with other kinds of behaviour or knowledge? I think it is probably fair to say that most linguists would agree that there are indeed such differences which make language different from everything else; but it is also true to say that various neighbouring disciplines (such as anthropology) have found the theories of linguistics a fruitful source of theories associated with things other than language. For example, I once read a book by an anthropologist about members of an African tribe who paint their bodies in various intricate patterns, in which he wrote a 'grammar' for these patterns modelled on the grammars for English that one particular school of linguists was writing at that time. If people working on things other than language can see similarities between their data and language, we may assume that the differences between language and other things cannot be overwhelming, and I for one am particularly impressed by these similarities.

The kind of question in which linguists are interested has to do with the general organization of language as well as with the particular categories of which language makes use. Examples of the latter would be 'noun', 'preposition', 'subjunctive' and 'voiced' (a phonetic term which I explained earlier). It seems unlikely that we should be able to find uses for any of these particular categories outside language, though the phonetic one could be used (for example) in the classification of wheezes by people with sore throats. However, if we raise the discussion to a more general level, we can see each of these terms as the name for a class of

144

objects (in this case, words or sounds), and as such they are by no means peculiar to language – indeed, any concept (such as 'mushroom') can be taken as referring to a class of objects. This takes us back to the question of whether language is organized in a unique way; and we can say that at least one part of the organization of language is commonplace, namely the part responsible for classifying bits of language.

When we look at other aspects of the organization of language, however, the answers are not always so obvious because we first have to decide how language is in fact organized before we can compare its organization with that of other things; and this means that we have to work out a satisfactory general theory of the organization of language. As I explained in chapter 7, there is a wide choice of theories, each purporting to be satisfactory and each (apparently) different in important respects from the others. This means that a comparison of language with other things, with regard to internal organization, will lead to different answers according to which of these theories we assume; so the debate about the uniqueness of language looks set to continue for some time to come.

CAN OTHER ANIMALS SPEAK?

It all depends on what you mean by 'speak'. A parrot can speak in the sense of being able to produce recognizable spoken words, but it has no idea what they mean and couldn't recombine them to make a different sentence, so there is less similarity than difference between the 'speaking' of parrots and that of humans. With various other animals the similarities increase, though (not surprisingly) it is a matter of debate whether they are sufficient for us to say 'Such-and-such animals can speak', using 'speak' in the same sense as when we apply it to human beings. Intensive research has been conducted recently into the behaviour of animals like dolphins, chimpanzees and gorillas to find out to what extent they can be taught something sufficiently similar to a human language to be called a human language (with negligible

145

differences, such as the fact that chimpanzees cannot produce suitable noises, so they need to use some other kind of medium, such as coloured chips of plastic).

Why does it matter? In a sense it doesn't, because there are probably few or no practical consequences either way. As far as I know nobody is suggesting that if we find that some species of animals can talk, then we shall have to start treating them as human beings – e.g. prosecuting them for going round without clothes on (though it could be argued that we ought to treat the higher animals better than we sometimes do). However, it is important for us to have a realistic view of our relations to the animal world because we all do have some view of these, and it is better for them to be realistic than unrealistic. And one of the most important differences which most of us see between ourselves and animals is that they are 'dumb' and we aren't. Souls, minds and feelings are other things which are commonly believed to be properties unique to human beings; each such belief may or may not be true. It is hard to imagine a research programme connected with the existence of souls, but by comparison the question of language is quite straightforward, and research is proceeding apace. We shall see later that there are other reasons as well for wanting to know the answer.

ARE THERE RACIAL DIFFERENCES IN LANGUAGE?

This question is about the connection between racial differences and language: do we find that particular races use particular languages or particular kinds of languages? In general, the answer is fairly clear: there is no known connection between a person's racial classification and any characteristic of his or her language. That is, a child of any racial background whatsoever may learn any language whatsoever if he or she is brought up in a community that speaks the language in question. We all know that this is true from seeing immigrant children learning an English which is indistinguishable from that of children born to long-established English-speaking families. This observation conflicts with the quite widely held view that some races are incapable of producing certain sounds because of the shape of their mouths (e.g. that Negroes can't produce some sounds because they have thick lips).

I think linguists would generally agree on this point, though it has to be admitted that it could be because we simply don't know enough about the more abstract features of language, and nobody has seriously tried to compare the distribution of racial and linguistic features. The one exception I know of is that there seems to be a connection within Europe between the distribution of a particular gene and the occurrence of the *th*-sound found in *thin*; at present this finding has not led to any kind of explanation, and linguists generally ignore it, assuming that it is simply the result of a chance similarity between the occurrence of two things which have no inherent connection.

For the time being, then, we may assume that none of the differences between languages is due to genetic differences between the communities that speak them.

ARE WE BORN TO SPEAK?

To judge by some books, you might well come to the conclusion that this is the only issue that linguists consider worth debating these days. The question is whether we are genetically programmed specifically to learn language – that is, whether our minds are shaped by our genes in such a way that we are born knowing something about language – or whether we are left to work it all out for ourselves by means of our general intelligence. The idea that we might be so programmed is not as far-fetched as it might seem, since plenty of animals are known to be born with quite specific skills and items of knowledge programmed into their brains – spiders which know how to build webs, birds and fish which know when and where to migrate and so on. So we cannot reject the idea out of hand – nor, of course, can we accept it without compelling evidence. A good deal of recent work on linguistic theory has attempted to provide just such evidence.

147

Put in somewhat oversimplified form, the research programme needed to produce the evidence is as follows. First
you decide how language is organized by studying a wide
range of languages in some detail and working out what they
all have in common. Then you find out how children learn
things from their experience – how they learn about places,
foods, people and so on. Then you put these two sets of
findings together and work out whether it would be possible
for children to learn the characteristics of language simply on
the basis of their experience. If the answer is 'yes', then there
is no need to assume any special genetic preparation for
learning language; if it is 'no', it follows that general learning
ability plus experience are not sufficient to explain how we
manage to learn a language. It would be reasonable, then, to
assume that the missing element is some kind of genetic
program which we have inherited from our ancestors.

It will probably be a long time before linguists are able to
arrive at anything approaching consensus on this question.
Before then we shall have to agree on what the general
properties of language are, and psychologists will have to
agree on how we learn things other than language. Some
linguists are already satisfied that we know enough about
both things to be able to say that we are born to speak –
we must be genetically programmed. Among these linguists
is Noam Chomsky – indeed, it is because of his skill in
arguing his case on this particular point that he is so famous
outside linguistics. Other linguists (perhaps even a majority,
though it is hard to tell) prefer to reserve judgement.

It is interesting to note that if Chomsky and his followers
are right, then at least some of the similarities between
languages are due to similarities in the genetic make-up of
their speakers, but none of the differences is due to genetic
differences (that is, if we accept the provisional conclusion
that we reached in the last section). This position seems
somewhat paradoxical if you think of the ways in which other
genetically programmed aspects of the human being vary
between communities (I have in mind things like skin colour
and shape of face); but no doubt there are many ways in
which the paradox could turn out to be illusory (e.g. it might

turn out that there are differences between languages which are due to genetic differences).

HOW OLD IS LANGUAGE?

The oldest written records known to us are those produced by the Sumerians in Mesopotamia about 5,000 years ago, but we can be sure that spoken language has been around for much longer than that. After all, it is obvious that writing was used in order to write something down and that something (spoken language) must have existed before writing was invented. So when did spoken language start? The simple answer is that we just don't know and probably never will know with any certainty – nor, for that matter, do we know how it started. The best we can do is to make guesses, while recognizing that any guess depends on a long chain of assumptions, any one of which may be wrong and may therefore invalidate the whole argument.

One approach makes use of fossilized remains of pre-historic people. Although we obviously can't tell directly whether these people used language, we can investigate the fossil remains relevant to their mouths and throats and work out what range of sounds they could have produced. This will give us some idea of the number of sounds they could contrast with one another, which we could then compare with the numbers of such sounds found in modern languages (between about twenty and seventy: English has about forty). If we could show that some particular set of fossil remains belonged to people who could make only a handful of distinct sounds, we could conclude that they must have had either a very limited vocabulary or very, very long words (since if words are to be distinct and you're short of distinct sounds, length is the only other variable). Either way, their language, if they had one, would have been noticeably different from a modern language. Conversely, if we found that their mouths and throats were similar to ours, then it remains at least possible that they had a language similar to ours as well. However, even the negative evidence of the first kind would

149

not be conclusive because language may well have started off as a system of gestures rather than noises and may have been transferred to the voice from the hands only after many of the essential characteristics of language had been developed. Many scholars take this possibility seriously these days, partly as a result of a series of studies by linguists of the sign languages used by deaf people.

Another approach makes use of the archaeological evidence for the culture and social organization of prehistoric peoples. As the evidence becomes more meagre, of course, speculation takes over, but at least it is limited to some extent by the facts. For example, there is evidence that humans (or near-humans) were using fire in their cave homes in China half a million years ago. When you think of the organization needed to keep a communal fire going, it is hard to avoid the conclusion that there must have been quite complex discussion of who was to gather wood, what kind of wood was best, how the fire should be damped down for the night and so on. From this guess you move to the assumption that there must have been quite a sophisticated system for communication – i.e. a language (whether of gesture or of sounds).

A third approach rests on the assumption that Chomsky is right and that humans all share the same genetic programs for language. If this is so, it must be that we have all inherited them from the same source, so we must ask when the most recent common ancestor community for the whole human race existed. This question pushes discussion of the age of our modern 'linguistic' genes back a very long time indeed, and we can presumably make the further assumption that this common ancestor community had not only 'linguistic' genes but also language. But all this depends, as we have seen, on whether or not Chomsky is right; if he isn't, we clearly can't attack the problem in this way.

This selection of questions raised by linguistics shows that there are a few to which linguists can give answers with some confidence and a large number about which the only honest thing to say at present is that we just don't know. However, the exciting thing about these cases is that although we don't know the answers, it is possible to imagine research which could lead us – or, more likely, our distant descendants – to them. You may think that is cold comfort for the present generation, including you, but you will find that the lack of clear answers doesn't spoil the fun of trying to think about the questions. Moreover, it is an imporant part of education to learn to consider radical alternatives to the fundamental assumptions you already hold, irrespective of whether or not you can actually decide between the alternatives; and you have probably noticed, in following the discussion in this chapter, that you already have some beliefs about most of the questions we have discussed. Whatever the merits of the views I have aired, they are probably at least as well founded as the views you started with.

9

Some Applications

Finally, I shall discuss some of the ways in which the findings of linguistics can be useful. I have already tried to show that the activity of studying linguistics can be good for you in itself because of the way in which it trains you to solve problems and think about complex social issues (among other things); I shan't repeat the point in the present chapter. Here we are concerned with ways in which the actual content of linguistics can be useful.

I shall structure the discussion by focusing on a number of types of people who can benefit from knowing some of this content, and you will see that many of the 'types' will be particular professions – teachers, doctors and so on. This may well suggest to you that a degree in linguistics might in itself count as a professional training for some career, but this is not so. Apart from a career as an academic linguist (which I haven't even bothered to list because there are so few professional openings), there are no careers for which a degree in linguistics would be a sufficient specific training. But what I shall show is that an intelligent understanding of the content of linguistics is of great value in a number of careers, so if you had the necessary professional training for those careers and linguistics as well, you would do the job much better than you would without the linguistics. Moreover, the normal professional training for many of these careers includes a substantial training in linguistics; this fact reflects the growing acceptance of the subject's importance in the professions concerned – and of course it means that if you went on to take such a course after a degree in linguistics, you would be able to do the linguistics components much more easily (or would even be exempted from them altogether).

The following are the types of people I shall discuss: citizens – i.e. anybody, irrespective of his or her job; parents – again, irrespective of their job; communicators – whether professional or not; teachers of any subject, of mother tongue or of second language; speech therapists and doctors concerned with speech disorders; translators; information processors; scholars in other disciplines. No doubt there are others that I could have included but haven't thought of. As it is, you will see from my comments that I know less about some of the professional applications than about others, but this doesn't matter too much, I hope, because if you are interested in any particular application you will in any case have to look at some more specialist literature.

CITIZENS

One thing that is fairly clear from research in linguistics is that language is like any other device which we humans find helpful (fire, machinery, atomic energy, etc.): it can be dangerous if not controlled intelligently. Accordingly, the better we understand how it works, the better we shall be able to control it.

One of the dangers of language is one on which I have already put quite a bit of stress in this book, namely the way in which language is used as a clue to a person's 'social identity' – we listen to people speaking and draw conclusions about their region of origin, job, educational background and so on. (In Britain this is done largely on the basis of pronunciation, which is perhaps less important in some other countries; but it is probably true of any complex community that social identity is signalled by linguistic differences, whether these involve pronunciation, vocabulary, syntax or complete language systems.)

It is very useful to be able to use language in this way when we meet strangers because their language gives us a lot of extra information about them, and this in turn allows us to predict their behaviour. Without such information, social interaction with strangers would be very difficult indeed. Imagine, for example, that you have to telephone a business in order to make an inquiry; you ring the number, and a voice answers you – but you don't know whether the voice belongs to a telephone receptionist, a secretary, the boss's secretary or even the boss himself. Once you have listened to the voice for a few seconds, however, you can probably eliminate most of these possibilities and pitch your inquiry accordingly.

There are three dangers in using language in this way. The first is that the conclusions we draw about people on the basis of their speech (or writing, of course) may be wrong – you may think you're talking to a receptionist and find out, after some embarrassing cross-talk, that it's the boss herself. There are very few linguistic clues which are 100 per cent reliable signals of any social property, and it is important to be aware all the time that any guess you make on the basis of linguistic clues is just a guess and may be wrong.

Another danger is perhaps not quite so obvious: the link between the linguistic clues and the social properties may be quite arbitrary, just like the link between the pronunciation of a word and its meaning, but we may assume it to be natural in some sense. One example of this is the way British people typically think some accents are in themselves worse (ugly, slovenly, etc.) than others, so that they can be seen as (yet more) unfavourable qualities of those who speak with those accents, along with poverty, living in ugly environments and so on. It is unfair to criticize a Cockney for speaking Cockney, as though this were in itself a shortcoming. Instead, one should try hard to see linguistic differences as just that – differences, with nothing to choose between the alternatives from the point of view of quality. Another example is the way we link knowledge of educated vocabulary to intelligence and assume that the former is a signal of the latter, as though the ability to replace *get* by *obtain* were a sign of superior intelligence. This raises the danger that the educational system will get diverted from its real business, training pupils' intelligence and skills, into the less essential business of developing their knowledge of educated-sounding vocabulary.

It is easy to see how language can control our thinking about people because of its close connection with social identity, but less easy to see how to prevent it from doing so. However, it should be the case that a linguistic training will help because it encourages a more objective view of language. This takes us to our third source of dangers for the citizen: the fact that language influences our way of thinking about the world in general by 'packaging' the world and presenting it to us in one particular way rather than another. This relates to the points I made in the last chapter about the link between language and culture, where I suggested that the existence in English of the word *toadstool* leads English speakers to the concept of 'toadstool', whereas the German language does not have this effect on its speakers (though, of course, it is possible that some German speakers may develop the concept for other reasons).

It may be that this particular example does not show language as a source of danger, though it could be argued that it prevents English speakers from eating more than a very limited range of fungus types. Take a different example: the word *cold*, as applied to an illness. According to medical opinion, the common cold is caused by a virus and not by getting cold – indeed, there is very little connection with coldness. And yet we are all, presumably, inclined to connect 'catching cold' with 'getting cold' because the same word occurs in both expressions. So we try to avoid catching cold by doing irrelevant things like keeping warm, instead of more relevant tricks like avoiding stuffy rooms. A famous American linguist quoted an even more dramatic example of the dangers of being misled by language: he discovered that many people thought that so-called 'empty' petrol drums were literally empty and therefore inert; so they saw no risk in using naked lights near them and consequently tended to cause fires. This mistake arose, presumably, because of the ambiguity of *empty*: it can mean 'containing nothing at all' or 'containing none of whatever it is meant to contain'. The drums were indeed empty in the second sense but not in the first. Such shifts of meaning are often deliberately exploited in advertising and propaganda, and we should all be on our guard against them. Once again, it should be easier if you've had some training in the objective study and analysis of meaning.

There has been a good deal of emphasis in recent linguistic work on the sexist bias of languages like English, which constitutes another example of the way in which language can control, or at least influence, our thinking. The main problem is that English tends to be grossly unfair to females by encouraging us to present them as deviations from the male 'norm'. For example, we talk about the brotherhood of man (to embrace the whole of humanity), not the sisterhood of woman or even the siblinghood of people! The examples of bias in vocabulary can be multiplied over and over again (and indeed have been in a number of studies): so anyone interested in improving the situation will at least have to find a way of improving the vocabulary of English, which means, among other things, being aware of both the linguistic and the social pressures against such change.

However, the problem goes deeper than vocabulary and involves the system of pronouns: we are all taught in school to use *he* rather than *they* to refer back to a noun or pronoun of uncertain sex (e.g. 'When anybody analyses a sentence, he should do as follows . . .'). It is hard not to draw the conclusion from this ruling that a person is 'normally' male unless the contrary is specified, which implies that females are abnormal. It would certainly be better to encourage the use of the more colloquial *they* in such cases ('When anybody analyses a sentence, they should do as follows . . .') and perhaps even to extend it to cases where the pronoun refers to a noun (e.g. 'When a linguist analyses a sentence, they should do as follows . . .').

To summarize, I have presented a number of problems which arise from the fact that language can control our thinking both about people to whom we are listening and about the world in general. This control is on the whole beneficial, since it is one of the main means by which we learn the culture of our community and thereby benefit from the experience of previous generations. However, previous generations may also have got it wrong, and we may be in danger of perpetuating their errors if we allow ourselves to be influenced in an uncritical way by our language. So I conclude that every citizen ought to be made more consciously aware of how language works, so that *they* (note choice of pronoun!) can be less at its mercy.

PARENTS

One of the most fascinating parts of any child's development, for its parents and other onlookers, is the rapid growth of language. Linguists have paid a good deal of attention to the acquisition of language by children during the past two decades in particular – the interest in fact dates back much further – so now any course on linguistics is likely to offer you at least a meaty helping of research findings and theories about how it happens. There is no shortage of unsolved problems, but there are some agreed conclusions that any parent ought to know about.

The most important one is probably that there is no need for parents to teach their language to their children. Every child seems to know exactly what to do in order to get efficient at language, simply by observing other speakers and guessing the rules they are applying. (Exactly why children are so good at this is a matter of hot debate, as I mentioned in the chapter on great issues. Some linguists think children are genetically 'programmed' to do it; others disagree.) Any deliberate attempt by parents to teach the language system (i.e. the rules of syntax, the vocabulary and so on) is likely to be at best a waste of time and, quite possibly, an unnecessary source of friction between parent and child. The fact is that even experts are largely in the dark about how children learn their language when it comes down to details, so no parent is likely to know enough about the child's way of learning to be able to guide it by teaching.

Having picked out this one general point, it is hard to select others for special mention here because there are so many equally good candidates – the fact that two equally normal, bright children may start speaking at different ages, the fact that children may 'know' adult forms but use different ones themselves (e.g. they understand *taught* but say *teached*), the fact that different children tend to follow very similar patterns of development (e.g. when they start using *not* they put it at the start of the sentence: *not Teddy asleep*, for 'Teddy isn't asleep') and so on and on. The more you, as a parent, know about the current state of research into language acquisition, the more fun it is to watch your own children.

Moreover, it would be wrong to conclude, from my earlier remarks about the uselessness of teaching language to children, that there is nothing that parents can do to positively help their children. On the contrary, there is probably a good deal because children seem to develop at different speeds, according to the kind of experience of language they have at home. For example, it may be particularly helpful to the child if the parent discusses the whys and wherefores of activities in which the child is actively involved. If this is so, then parents ought to know what kinds of activity are especially helpful for the child's linguistic development.

COMMUNICATORS

The processes involved in communication are more complex than most of us realize, and linguistics is one of the main disciplines which contribute to our understanding of them. Even an apparently straightforward exchange between two friends will turn out to be unexpectedly complicated. For example, if he says to her, 'I can't do this problem', she may well take it as a request for help, although he hasn't actually said, 'I want you to help me.' A good deal more is communicated than we actually put into words, so a theoretical study of how communication takes place must sort out the various contributions made by literal meaning and the various implications that can be worked out on the basis of everything else that the hearer knows. Moreover, even what is put into words may be put more or less directly – for instance, he could have said, 'I can't do this wretched problem', from which she could infer that he was fed up with the problem, although he hasn't actually said as much.

Most of us are reasonably successful at communicating about straightforward topics with people we know well, but the problems multiply as the situations get more rarefied – for example, when you are writing an essay it is often not at all clear whom you are addressing, which means that you don't know what knowledge you can take for granted; and when you are issuing official orders on notices it isn't even clear who you are supposed to be (yourself, or the whole organization on whose behalf you are issuing the notice, or some disembodied abstract personification of it, or what?). In most cases it is possible to work out rationally what you are trying to do and then to work out the most efficient means of doing it, given the means at your disposal. This work of analysis is likely to be easier for you if you can work within some general theory of communication and language, and it may well be that you will find that your solution is different from the conventions to which you have been accustomed. For instance, there is a general convention that writers should avoid referring to themselves or to their readers, so they should avoid using *I* and *you*, but I can see very little justification for this convention, so I have ignored it, as you may have noticed.

Of course, there are professional communicators, called journalists, advertisers, writers and 'the media', and such people naturally have to take a professional approach to their business. There are professional courses to train them in the solving of communication problems, and the findings of linguistics are bound to be an important part of what they have to learn.

TEACHERS

It is often said that every teacher is a teacher of the mother tongue (which I shall assume, for simplicity, to be English), and there is a good deal of truth in this, if only because every teacher teaches technical terminology relating to his or her own subject. However, it goes beyond this, because every teacher acts as a linguistic model for pupils and at least has the opportunity to comment on pupils' own linguistic efforts (an opportunity which is often exploited). Because of this there is increasing pressure on the colleges where teachers train to ensure that every teacher follows a course on language, in which such things are discussed in connection with the role of language in learning. (In Britain the pressure has had considerable effect on the training of primary schoolteachers but somewhat less on that of secondary teachers.)

It is even more obvious that the findings of linguistics are relevant to teachers whose first concern is language – primary teachers dealing with reading and writing, secondary teachers of 'English', teachers of foreign languages like French and teachers of English as a second language for minority language groups. All such teachers need two things which linguists can supply: a general theory of language and a body of facts about particular languages.

Take primary schoolteachers. They need to understand clearly what the relation is between speech and writing because of their concern with the teaching of reading and writing; and this understanding needs to be quite substantial, not just a matter of generalities. For example, can they assume that the child already 'knows' about sentence boundaries, in the sense in which it already knows about the word *cat* before it learns to write it? In addition, they need to know a lot about the English spelling system, so as to be able to explain it where appropriate, and also a good deal about the specific differences between what the child already knows, as a speaker of whatever the local kind of English is, and what needs to be learned about standard written English. All this requires quite a sophisticated and detailed familiarity with some parts of linguistics. And, of course, since the child at primary school is still in the process of acquiring language, the teacher also needs to understand how this takes place and how best to help the child, just as a parent does.

Other kinds of language teacher have comparable, though different, needs which linguistics can satisfy, but there is probably no need to give examples. What is becoming increasingly clear is that there is a great deal of overlap between the contents of the different kinds of language teaching; for example, all of them require the teacher to adopt some kind of position on the relations between spoken and written language, and all of them are greatly improved if the teacher has a clear idea of how the child's ordinary language differs from standard English, French or whatever kind of language is being taught. Some educationalists question the way in which these kinds of language teaching are divided up, at least in most British schools, and are suggesting that schools might have a department of language, which would bring together all the teachers responsible for language and encourage them to colaborate and present a unified view of language. Any such change would, of course, tend to increase the influence of linguistics in schools – as would any move towards the teaching of linguistics as a part of the school curriculum, which I hinted at in an earlier chapter.

SPEECH THERAPISTS AND DOCTORS CONCERNED WITH SPEECH DISORDERS

Some unfortunate people suffer from language disorders of one kind or another, ranging from lisps and stammering to complete loss of the ability to speak. The medical profession includes a body of specialists in such disorders, namely speech therapists and certain kinds of doctor. It is obvious that linguistics has an essential contribution to make to their work, since a disorder can't even be described without making use of sophisticated linguistic analysis, and proper diagnosis and cure require a very profound understanding of how language works in general and of how the patient's language has been affected.

TRANSLATORS

Translation raises important questions about the nature of language which we have already touched upon as one of our great issues. Anyone who has done translation knows that there is more than one way of translating any given text into another language, so it is helpful for a translator to have a classification of translation types to which he can refer. We have a distinction between 'literal' and 'loose' translation, but this is extremely crude, and a working translator needs a much more sophisticated set of terminology to use, for example, when negotiating with a client about the kind of translation he or she wants. This classification presupposes a theory of translation (several of which already exist) – which in turn presupposes a sophisticated theory of language, as provided by linguistics.

As I have mentioned (see chapter 2), the possibility of translating by computer is gradually turning into a reality, though the systems that exist at present are still fairly limited. The problems to be overcome are enormous because of the sheer quantity of information which the computer has to be able to make use of if it is to match the performance of a human translator. Imagine that you had to translate the sentence *Cheese sandwiches are filling* into some other language. You may be under the impression that this would be a straightforward job, on the assumption that the other language contains words for *cheese*, for *sandwich* and for *filling*, but this is not so. You are already at the stage in the analysis of the English sentence where you understand exactly what it means, but this is itself the result of a mass of complex thinking by you, which all took place as you were reading the sentence. And this thinking has to be matched by the computer if it is to reach your present state of understanding of the English language; and all this must happen before it starts to work out a roughly equivalent sentence in another language.

To make this point clear, let us take your understanding operation in slow motion. First, you read the word *cheese* (for the moment we must ignore the fact that your eyes actually read more than one word at a time); then comes *sandwiches*, giving you *cheese sandwiches* to process. Now, one problem is that very many English words can be used either as nouns or as verbs, and *sandwich* is one of them; so you could take *sandwiches* either as a plural noun, with *cheese* modifying it, or as a present-tense verb, with *cheese* as its subject (compare *cheese tastes nice* or even *cheese sandwiches things well*, if you can ignore the difficulty of supplying a context). When you have decided (perhaps on the basis of the next word, *are*) that *sandwiches* is a noun, you still have to decide what the meaning of the pair *cheese sandwiches* is. Is it like *jam sandwiches*, where *jam* defines the filling, or *brown-bread sandwiches*, where *brown-bread* defines the outer layers? You decide on the former, partly because you know that cheese is typically used as a filling and not as an outer layer. But this knowledge is part of your general knowledge rather than something you would expect to find in a dictionary for English; so the computer would have to 'know' a lot not only about the English language but also about English culture (e.g. what goes into sandwiches).

Linguistics has a very important part to play in the development of successful computer programs for translating, though, as we have just seen, many other disciplines also need to be involved. Linguists will have to provide the necessary theory of language structure and part of the theory of communication (e.g. of how we make use of general knowledge), and it will also have to provide a mass of details about the vocabulary, syntax, inflections, etc., of the languages concerned.

INFORMATION PROCESSORS

It is often said that the last few decades have witnessed an 'information explosion' which is almost as dramatic as the population explosion, and we see figures to substantiate the claim, such as the number of new scientific journals which are launched per day, taking the world as a whole. Even within a relatively small discipline like linguistics the number of books and articles published each year is already well beyond the capacity of any individual to read everything, and even if you specialize in one specific area of linguistics (e.g. the syntax of English), you are likely to have trouble keeping up with the literature. The problem is clear: an important discovery may be made and reported in a publication, but if the report isn't read by the people who might find it relevant, it may as well not have been made, and the effort that produced it is wasted.

Once again, computers may provide at least a partial solution to the problem, which typically takes the form of a researcher wanting to know the 'state of the art' on some fairly specialized topic and not knowing even what articles or books have been written about it, let alone what they say. In some disciplines it is already possible to exploit a computer-held reservoir of information, in which books and articles are simply classified according to the topics with which they deal. Thus, by specifying the topics concerned, our researcher can get the computer to print out a list of the relevant publications that are in its reservoir.

However, the system I have just described isn't ideal. For one thing, it requires an expensive team of experts to provide the reservoir of classified literature; for another, it requires them to make subtle judgements about what exactly some book is 'about'. For example, if half a page of some book on linguistics is devoted to an original and important discussion of one particular word, would the classifiers say that the book was 'about' that word (among other things)? Another problem is that the system presupposes some particular list of topics, which must remain unchanged, since it is the fixed point of reference for the whole system, so the particular topic in which the researcher is interested may not be included among the listed ones; and, more generally, the research interests of the whole community of scholars may shift from one decade to the next. Finally, our researcher still has the task of getting hold of the books and articles on his reading list and then of reading them all to find out what they say. And, of course, the more comprehensively the system covers the literature, the longer the reading list will be, so the researcher may well end up with a good year's solid reading as a result of the computer's efficiency.

Wouldn't it be good if a computer could do the entire job for us? The scenario to be imagined is as follows: all publications are produced on computer-readable tapes (or discs, or whatever), and their actual contents (not just their titles) are included in the central reservoir of information. Then when you come up with a research topic and want to know the 'state of the art', you don't ask the computer for a list of the relevant publications, but instead you ask it for a summary of the state of knowledge about the subject concerned. The computer would be able to provide this summary because it would have analysed all the texts in the reservoir and extracted the information contained in them; so it would have an up-to-date 'general knowledge' based on the total literature for the discipline concerned. All that would remain would be for the computer to produce a coherent account, in prose, of what it knows about the specified topic.

A total system like the one described is science fiction at present, but the component parts are not. The kind of processing of texts needed would be similar to the processing needed for translation by computer described above, and, as I said there, some progress has already been made in this area. Progress has also been made in the storing and updating of general knowledge by computer and in getting computers to produce prose texts in reply to questions from an operator. So all that is needed is more progress in these areas and then a vast integrating operation. The point of interest here is that linguistics will be essential at various stages in the development of the system, especially at the stages dealing with the analysis and understanding of incoming texts and with the production of prose output.

SCHOLARS IN OTHER DISCIPLINES

Many other disciplines look to linguistics for help (just as linguistics benefits from their expertise) apart from the areas already mentioned (educators, speech pathologists, computer scientists, information scientists and so on). Psychologists hope linguists will be able to help them to explore the part of our minds (or even brains) that deals with language; philosophers want help in exploring the nature of meaning (and other matters); literary experts stand to benefit from what linguists can tell them about style, the nature of linguistic structures found in poetry and so on; anthropologists use language as a clue to culture, so they are interested in what linguists have to say about meaning and culture. The list could be extended to a number of other disciplines. The picture is not always like the one I have suggested here: linguists sometimes pay less attention than they should to what is going on in neighbouring disciplines, and the latter sometimes reciprocate. Nevertheless, it is clear that many of the findings of linguistics are potentially relevant, and important, for other disciplines.

Apart from the suggestions for further reading and the glossary, that is the end of what I want to tell you about linguistics. I hope that what I have said here has helped you to decide whether or not linguistics is for you. It would be unrealistic for me to claim that it is the ideal subject for everyone, and you may have decided by now that you don't really want to spend any more of your life on linguistics and that some other subject appeals much more. In that case, I thank you for your attention and hope you don't regret the time you gave me. Naturally, though, I shall be pleased if I have managed to persuade you that the scientific study of language need be neither woolly speculation nor dry-as-dust pedantry but can combine the rigour of natural science with the personal interest of the humanities.

Further Reading

Over the past decade or so quite a number of introductory books on linguistics have been published. Depending on your personal tastes and interests, you will find some of them stimulating and illuminating and others too superficial, too advanced or just plain boring. I cannot make this choice for you, and in any case most books have good and bad mixed up together, so you will probably have to put up with what you find and skip energetically. Not all of the following books will be easy for you to get hold of; your choice will be limited to a large extent by the stock of your local library, the size and efficiency of your bookshop and the current state of publishers' stock lists.

GENERAL

Aitchison, J., *Teach Yourself Linguistics*, Sevenoaks, Hodder & Stoughton, 1978

Akmajian, A., Demers, R. A., and Harnish, R. M., *Linguistics: An Introduction to Language and Communication*, London, MIT Press, 1979

Atkinson, M., Kilby, D., and Rocca, I., *Foundations of General Linguistics*, London, Allen & Unwin, 1982

Bolinger, D., and Sears, M. (eds.), *Aspect of Language*, 3rd edn, New York, Harcourt, Brace, Jovanovich, 1980

Crystal, D., *Linguistics*, Harmondsworth, Penguin, 1971

Fromkin, V., and Rodman, R., *An Introduction to Language*, 2nd edn, New York, Holt, Rinehart & Winston, 1978

Lyons, J., *Language and Linguistics*, Cambridge, Cambridge University Press, 1981

Simpson, J. M. Y., *A First Course in Linguistics*, Edinburgh, Edinburgh University Press, 1979

PARTICULAR AREAS OF STRUCTURAL LINGUISTICS

Leech, G., *Semantics*, Harmondsworth, Penguin, 1982

Lyons, J., *Chomsky*, London/Glasgow, Fontana, 1977

O'Connor, J. D., *Phonetics*, Harmondsworth, Penguin, 1973

Palmer, F., *Grammar*, Harmondsworth, Penguin, 1971

Potter, S., *Our Language*, Harmondsworth, Penguin, 1950

Smith, N. V. S., and Wilson, D., *Modern Linguistics: The Results of Chomsky's Revolution*, Harmondsworth, Penguin, 1979

SOCIAL ASPECTS OF LANGUAGE

Aitchison, J., *Language Change: Progress or Decay?*, London, Hutchinson, 1981

Burling, R., *Man's Many Voices: Language in its Cultural Context*, New York, Holt, Rinehart & Winston, 1970

Farb, P., *Word Play: What Happens When People Talk*, Sevenoaks, Hodder & Stoughton, 1973

Trudgill, P., *Sociolinguistics*, Harmondsworth, Penguin, 1974

PSYCHOLOGICAL ASPECTS OF LANGUAGE

Aitchison, J., *The Articulate Mammal*, London, Hutchinson, 1976

Greene, J., *Thinking and Language*, London, Methuen, 1975

SOME APPLICATIONS

Bolinger, D., *Language: The Loaded Weapon – the Use and Abuse of Language Today*, London, Longman, 1980

Further Reading

Carter, R. (ed.), *Linguistics and the Teacher*, London, Routledge & Kegan Paul, 1982

Corder, P., *Applied Linguistics*, Harmondsworth, Penguin, 1978

Trudgill, P., *Accent, Dialect and the School*, London, Arnold, 1975

Glossary

This glossary contains terms that are used in this book and isn't meant as a guide to all possible uses of the terms – a general fact about language is that many words have more than one meaning, and the same is true of linguistic terminology as well. And I have tried to give not rigorous, watertight definitions but rather examples and hints. If you want better definitions and a fuller list, you won't be able to improve on D. Crystal's *A First Dictionary of Linguistics and Phonetics* (London, André Deutsch, 1980).

ADJECTIVE	A descriptive word like *big*, which can be attached to a NOUN (*a big boy*) or used after a VERB like *be* or *seem* (*he seems big*) and may itself have a word like *very* attached to it (*very big*)
AFFIX	A part of a word which is connected with the word's meaning or SYNTAX but is not a ROOT (e.g. *-s* and *-ing* in *come-s* and *com-ing*); an affix may be a PREFIX, an INFIX or a SUFFIX
APPOSITION	The relation between pairs of words like *friend* and *John* in *my friend John*
ARTICLE	The words *the* ('definite' article) and *a/an* ('indefinite' article)
ASSIMILATE	If one sound (A) occurs together with another sound (B) and A has replaced a different sound which was less similar

170

Glossary

to B than A is, then we say that this sound has been 'assimilated' to B

AUXILIARY VERB A VERB such as *be, have* or *can* which is used with another verb (e.g. *is going, have gone, can go*) and has certain SYNTACTIC peculiarities (e.g. taking *– n't*, as in *isn't going*)

CASE (FORM) If a word has different forms (e.g. *I/me*) according to how it is related to the rest of the sentence, these different forms are called 'cases' or 'case forms'

CLAUSE A group of words centring on a VERB (e.g. *the sun shone brightly*)

CLICK A sound used in some languages as an ordinary CONSONANT but used in English for expressing disapproval, talking to horses, etc. One example of a click sound is often written in English as *tut-tut*

COGNATE Words that are linked through time with a single word in some earlier language (e.g. French *père* and Spanish *padre*, both being descended from the Latin word *patrem*, 'father')

CONSONANT A sound or letter like *b, f, s, m, l*, which can't make up the whole of a word and, when pronounced, requires some kind of audible blockage in the mouth

CONSTRUCTION A pattern of words such as a GRAMMAR would discuss; e.g. we can identify (at least) two contructions in *Small babies sleep*: one involving *small* and *babies*, and the other involving *sleep* and the whole of *small babies* (or possibly just *babies*)

DESCRIPTIVE The analysis and description of particular languages or the objective and non-evaluative study of language (compare PRESCRIPTIVE)

DIACHRONIC ANALYSIS	The analysis of language over time; see HISTORICAL LINGUISTICS
DIALECT	A variety of a language, such as London English or standard English
DIRECT OBJECT	In *I gave the cat some fish, some fish* is classified as the direct OBJECT, and *the cat* as indirect object
ETYMOLOGY	The study of the historical origins of words
GENDER	A way of classifying the NOUNS of a language which relates to a sex-based classification of the objects to which they refer, though the connection with sex is often only approximate
GLOTTAL STOP	A sound like a little 'pop' made in the throat (often called a 'catch') which in some languages is used as a CONSONANT but in others occurs just before word-initial VOWELS when these are stressed particularly strongly (e.g. in many DIALECTS of English)
GRAMMAR	The study of SYNTAX and MORPHOLOGY and possibly also SEMANTICS or a book produced as the result of this study
GRAMMATICAL RELATIONS	Relations like SUBJECT and OBJECT, which would be mentioned in a GRAMMAR
HISTORICAL LINGUISTICS	The study of how languages change through time and of how languages are related to one another as a result of such change
INFINITIVE	A subclass of VERBS which in English have no SUFFIX at all but which in some other languages have special suffixes (e.g. *-er* in French *porter*). Sometimes the *to* which precedes the English infinitive is included as part of the infinitive (e.g. *to come*)
INFIX	A type of AFFIX which occurs inside the

172

	ROOT, of which there are no examples in English or other well-known Western European languages
INFLECTION	The part of a word (e.g. an AFFIX) that shows its NUMBER, TENSE, etc. (e.g. the -*s* of *dogs* is an inflection)
INTONATION	The musical pattern that is imposed on a sentence
LINGUIST	One who studies and analyses language(s)
LINGUISTICS	The professional activities of a LINGUIST
MAIN VERB	The VERB in a CLAUSE which can occur on its own (e.g. in *John lost the match although he played well*, *John lost the match* can occur without *although he played well*, but not vice versa, so *lost* is the main verb)
METALANGUAGE	Technical terminology that LINGUISTS use for talking about language
MODIFIER	A word that depends on another word (its 'head') for its links with the rest of the sentence (e.g. in *small people play well*, *small* is the modifier of *people* and *well* is the modifier of *play* because their positions are fixed in relation to *people* and *play* respectively)
MORPHOLOGY	The study of the internal STRUCTURE of words – how they are made up of smaller parts, such as AFFIXES and ROOTS – to the extent that this is related to SYNTAX or SEMANTICS
NON-STANDARD	A type of DIALECT which is not taken as a STANDARD
NOUN	A class of words which includes (*inter alia*) those that refer to concrete items (*desk*) and individual people (*John*)
NUMBER	The distinction between SINGULAR and PLURAL
OBJECT	A word or PHRASE which is attached to

a VERB but which is not its SUBJECT (or various other possibilities) (e.g. *apples* in *I like apples, She eats apples*)

PAST TENSE
A form of a VERB which refers to an event that has happened before the moment of speaking

PERSON
The distinction between *I/we* ('first person' SINGULAR and PLURAL), *you* ('second person' SINGULAR and PLURAL), *he/she/it* ('third person' SINGULAR and *they* ('third person' PLURAL)

PHONETICS
The study of sounds made in speaking, especially when these are studied without reference to the way in which they are used in particular languages

PHONOLOGY
The study of sounds made in speaking, especially when these are considered as part of the total STRUCTURE of particular languages

PHRASE
A group of words centring on a word other than a VERB (e.g. *in bed, the book* – compare CLAUSE) or any group of words which carries meaning

PITCH
The musical characteristic ('high' or 'low') of a sound

PLOSIVE
A kind of CONSONANT sound made by blocking the flow of air completely then releasing the air again under pressure (e.g. *p, b, t, g*)

PLURAL
NOUNS may be classified as singular or plural; this is a classification needed for SYNTAX (e.g. for the contrast between *Cakes are nice* and *Cake is nice*), but it is related to the SEMANTIC classification of the things referred to as one or more than one, although the syntactic and semantic classifications don't always agree (e.g. *oats* is syntactically plural)

POLYGLOT	A person who can speak many languages
POSTPOSITION	A word like a PREPOSITION except that it occurs after the word or PHRASE which is attached to it rather than before it (e.g. English *ago*, German *gegenüber*)
POSSESSIVE	A word which indicates some kind of possession on the part of the person to which it refers (e.g. *John's* is possessive in *John's hat*)
PRAGMATICS	The study of language in relation to the way it is used, especially when this study focuses on meaning
PREFIX	A kind of AFFIX which occurs before the ROOT
PREPOSITION	A class of words defined in SYNTAX and including *in, of, with,* etc. Such words are syntactically different from NOUNS, VERBS and ADJECTIVES but occur with another word or phrase attached to them; unlike POSTPOSITIONS, prepositions precede this word or PHRASE
PRESENT TENSE	A form of a VERB which refers to an event occurring at the time of speaking (e.g. *see* in contrast to PAST TENSE *saw*)
PRESCRIPTIVE	An approach to language which regards some forms or varieties of language as less correct or good than others (compare DESCRIPTIVE)
PRONOUN	A type of NOUN which defines the thing (etc.) that it refers to only in terms of categories like GENDER, NUMBER, PERSON (e.g. *I, he, who, yourself*)
PSYCHOLINGUISTICS	The study of how people think and behave in relation to language, within the framework of cognitive psychology

ROOT	The main part of a word to which AFFIXES may be added; the root is the part which is listed in the dictionary (e.g. *dog*, as in *dog-s*)
SEMANTICS	The study of meaning, especially those parts of meaning which do not derive from the circumstances in which words are used (compare PRAGMATICS)
SINGULAR	The opposite of PLURAL
SOCIOLINGUISTICS	The study of speakers as members of communities and other groupings
SOUND CHANGE	Change in the pronunciation of words during the course of history
SPOONERISM	A slip of the tongue in which the initial sounds of two words occurring in the same sentence are interchanged (e.g. *tip of the slongue*)
STANDARD	A variety of a language which is used in writing and which is favoured in various national-level activities
STRESS	The force with which a sound is produced, affecting its loudness (e.g. the stressed SYLLABLE in *linguistics* is the second one)
STRUCTURAL LINGUISTICS	The modern type of linguistics which concentrates on studying the STRUCTURE of a language, or parts of the language in relation to this structure, rather than on studying parts atomistically without reference to one another
STRUCTURALIST LINGUISTICS	A now rather unfashionable school of linguistics which flourished in the United States in the 1950s
STRUCTURE	The total set of all the rules and words in a language, plus their interconnections, or of a sentence and the various patterns and words found in it (which may be studied as parts of PHONOLOGY, MORPHOLOGY, SYNTAX or SEMANTICS)

SUBJECT	A word or PHRASE which is attached to a VERB and normally precedes it
SUBJUNCTIVE	A syntactic class of VERB (in some languages, though probably not in English), which normally occurs subordinated ('subjoined') to another verb – i.e. not as a MAIN VERB (the best candidate in English is *were*, as in *if I were king*)
SUFFIX	A type of AFFIX which follows the ROOT
SYNCHRONIC ANALYSIS	The study of languages (compare DIACHRONIC) as they exist at particular moments of historical time, without reference to earlier stages
SYLLABLE	A VOWEL with or without a CONSONANT before or after it (e.g. there are three syllables in *banana*)
SYNTAX	The study of how words are combined with one another; compare MORPHOLOGY, GRAMMAR
TENSE	A distinction in GRAMMAR that is related to time (e.g. PAST TENSE, *I went*; PRESENT TENSE, *I go*; FUTURE TENSE, *I shall go*)
THEORETICAL LINGUISTICS	The study of language at the most general level (compare DESCRIPTIVE linguistics)
TYPOLOGY	The study of how languages differ from one another, with emphasis on the most general kinds of difference
UVULA	The little wobbly thing hanging down at the back of your mouth
VERB	A class of words (compare NOUN, ADJECTIVE, PREPOSITION) that includes words for events located in time, through the TENSE distinction (e.g. *left* is a verb in *John left early* and so is *leaves* in *John leaves early*)
VOCAL CORDS	The folds of skin in your throat which

produce the vibration that disting-
uishes *v* from *f*, for example, and
which gives sounds their PITCH

VOICE(LESS)

Voice is the vibration that is part of
some sounds but not others and is
made by the VOCAL CORDS; you can feel
it by putting your finger lightly against
your larynx (Adam's apple, if you have
one) and comparing *v* (which has
voice) with *f* (which is voiceless)

VOICED

A sound that contains VOICE

VOWEL

A speech sound that could make up a
complete SYLLABLE, such as *a* or *o*
(compare CONSONANT), made without
audible friction

Index

a/an, 59–60, 123–5
accent, 44, 50, 154; *see also*
    pronunciation
adjective, 85, 170
adverb, 85
advertising, 156
affix, 81, 85, 94–5, 170
Africa, 82, 83, 100
Amazon, 25–7
ambiguity, 110–16
and, 69
animal speech, 145–6
anthropology, 144, 166
apostrophe *'s,* 6–7, 22, 23
apposition, 79, 170
Arab grammarians, 2
Arabic, 10, 82, 83
arbitrariness, 19
archaeology, 149–50
article, 59–60, 170
assimilation, 101–5, 170
attitudes, 35, 40–1, 84, 154–5
Australia, 33, 43, 93–4

before, 110–16
Beja, 27, 82–5, 105–10
beliefs, 35, 48
Brazil, 25–7

case, 25, 79, 171
cease, 66
century, 60
change, 5–7, 118–23

Chinese grammarians, 2
Chomsky, Noam, 33, 129, 148, 150
class, social, 20–1, 43–5
classroom, language in the, 49–51
clause, 74, 110, 113, 171
click, 83, 103, 171
cognate, 122, 171
cold, 155
Colombia, 25–7
communication, 137–8, 158–9
comparative, 85
competence, 74
computers, 36–7, 162–5
concepts, 52; *see also* mind
consonant, 3, 9, 59–62, 124, 171
construction, 3, 171
creased, 46
culture, 89–95, 135–7, 142–4, 155,
    163
Cushitic, 82

diachronic, 6, 172
dialect, 40–2, 121, 172
dictionary, 9, 12, 34, 38, 74
disorders of language, 17, 53, 161
do/done, 8–9, 38, 41

education, 50; *see also* social class;
    schools, language teaching in
    efficiency of language, 132–5
empty, 155
English, 5, 6, 9–11, 21, 33–4,
    43–51, 58–77, 81, 110–16, 119

Index

English — *continued*
  standard 38–9, 54–5
  see also Scotland; United States of
    America; *also* throughout
enough, 139
Esperanto, 139
etymology, 10–11, 122–3, 172
euphony, 23
ever, 71

farm, 119–20
feminine, 79–80
four-letter word, 26, 46
French, 5, 40, 79–80, 97, 101–2, 121,
  123, 136–7, 160
function of language, 16
fungus, 143

gender, 70, 79–82, 172
generalization, 9–13, 24, 98–114
genetics, 33, 147–50, 157
germ, 141
German, 11, 122–3, 135–6, 143
Germany, 118–21
gestures, 150
get, 50, 154
glottal stop, 83–4, 94, 122, 172
go/went, 14, 35
graffiti, 46
grammar, 4, 5, 12, 75, 172
Greek grammarians, 2

have/has/'s, 10, 64–5, 123
h-dropping, 20, 22, 43, 124–5
Hebrew, 82
hotel, 125–6
hundred, 10

I/me, 68–9, 159
Indian grammarians, 2
infinitive, 66–8, 172
infix, 86, 172–3
inflection, 62–4, 74, 75, 85–7,
  105–10, 173
intonation, 84, 173
is/'s, 22–4, 42, 64–5
Italian, 88, 121

Japanese, 5
Japanese grammarians, 2

kinship, 89–94
knowledge of language, 54, 74,
  144–9; *see also* mind

language, problems of, 38–56,
  133–44, 152–66
languages, number of, 12
  differences among, 5, 24–7, 33–4,
    78–95, 142–3
  primitive, 33–4
larynx, 10, 62
Latin, 10, 88, 97–100, 121
learning of language, 26, 35, 40,
  53–4, 157–8, 160
lexical item, 74
linguist, 1, 173; *see also* polyglot
linguistics, 31
linguistics, definition of, 1, 173
  and time, 5–7
  and generality, 9–13
  as a science, 13–15, 123
  at tertiary level, 2
  branches of, 3–5
  controversy in, 15–17, 29
  descriptive, 7–9, 16, 118, 171
  historical, 5–7, 10–11, 79, 172; *see
    also* sound change
  history of, 2, 15, 33, 42
  in schools, 2
  names for, 3
  practical benefits of, 16–17,
    29–30, 35–7, 38–53
  prescriptive, 7–9, 16, 57, 175; *see
    also* normative grammar
  structural, 10, 176
  structuralist, 10, 176
  theoretical, 11, 118, 177
literary experts, 165–6
London, speech habits in, 20

masculine, 79–80
mathematics, 27, 29, 96, 111
meaning, 4, 6, 11, 16, 22–4, 28,
  30–2, 49–51, 65–6, 69–73, 74,
  89–95, 110–16

Index

metalanguage, 16, 173; *see also* terminology
mind, 4, 51–3, 147–9; *see also* thinking
modifier, 7, 74, 173
moiety, 93–4
mood, 79
morphology, 3, 62–4, 84–7, 173
mother tongue, 26

names, choice of, 26–7
negative, 86
neither, 71
never, 71
Njamal, 93–4
Nootka, 94–5
normative grammar, 16, 54, 57; *see also* linguistics, prescriptive
norms, 19–21
not/n't, 42, 64–5
notation, 1, 101, 111
noun, 6, 30–2, 79, 85, 110, 173
number, 70, 173

oats, 31
object (direct), 4, 5, 68–9, 79, 86–8, 172, 173–4
objectivity, 13–15
Old English, 7
one, 70
operator, 65, 76
our/us, 40

part of speech, 74, 78
past, 8–9, 14, 35, 40, 62–3, 72–3, 85, 174
people, 31
person, 70, 72, 174
philosophy, 165
phonetics, 3, 10, 101–3, 174
phonology, 3, 174
phrase, 74, 174
pitch, 84, 174
plosive, 10, 60, 174
plural, 4, 7, 30–2, 81, 174
polyglot, 1, 12, 175
postposition, 5, 175

possession, 6, 175
pragmatics, 4, 175
prefix, 175
preposition, 5, 175
prescriptivism, 42; *see also* linguistics, prescriptive
present, 72–3, 175
prestige, 54–5
problem-solving, 29, 96–116
pronoun, 68–9, 79, 156–7, 175
pronunciation, 3, 9, 20, 34, 43–5, 54–5, 58–62, 74, 82–4; *see also* sounds, sound change
propaganda, 156
psycholinguistics, 4, 140–4, 175
psychology, 165

queen, 10
question, 47, 64–5

race, 146–7
r-dropping, 20–2, 43, 119
relations, grammatical, 79, 172
relative clause, 85–9, 105–10
relativity, 19–21
Romance languages, 97, 121
Romanian, 121
root, 86, 176
rules, 8–9, 10–11, 19–21, 39–40, 42, 46, 55, 74, 96–114, 125; *see also* norms, relativity, sound change
Russian, 33, 88

Sapir, Edward, 94–5
scales, 31
schools, language teaching in, 7, 8, 19, 22, 38–42, 72, 79, 82, 159–61; *see also* classroom, language in the
Scotland, 20, 43
semantics, 4, 69–73, 176
Semitic, 82
sex, 70, 79, 90–4
sexism, 156
sheep, 31
sibling, 90, 135
sign language, 150
singular, 30–2, 176

Index

slang, 46–7
slip of the tongue, 51–3
social groups, 4–5, 34–5, 44–8, 54–5, 128–9
social structure, 33, 92–4
sociolinguistics, 4–5, 176
sound change, 10–11, 20–1, 118–23, 176
sounds, 3, 6, 9–10, 100–5, 149–50; *see also* pronunciation
Spanish, 79–80, 88, 97, 101–2, 121, 123
speaker, 70
speech, and writing, 53–4, 149–50
  casual, 7, 39, 54
  disorders of, 53
  planning of, 4, 51–3, 141–2
  skill in, 55
speech therapy, 53, 161
spelling, 9, 43–4, 54, 74, 106, 160
spoonerism, 51–2, 176
standard language, 8, 39–48, 160, 176
stop, 66
stress, 84, 97, 176
structure, 10, 16, 25, 74, 144–5, 148–9, 176
style, 6–7, 22, 38, 45–8, 50–1, 70, 94–5, 134
subject, 4, 64, 68–9, 74, 79, 88, 177
subjunctive, 177
Sudan, 27, 82
suffix, 7, 31, 86, 177
Sumerian, 149
superlative, 85
syllable, 59, 177
symbolism, 42–8, 153–4
synchronic, 6, 177
syntax, 3, 64–9, 74, 105–10, 177

taboo, *see* four-letter word
take/took, 35, 86
tariff, 10
Tass, 120
teaching, 16–17, 159–61; *see also* schools, language teaching in
teenagers, 46–7

tend, 67–8
tense, 8–9, 72–3, 79, 177; *see also* past
terminology, 13, 49
the, 125
theories, 11, 29–32, 80–2, 117–30, 144–5, 160–1
thinking, 32, 140–4, *see also* mind
this/these, 31–2
time, 5–7, 72–3, 110–16, 143
Transformational Generative Grammar, 129
translation, 135–8, 161–3
try, 40, 46, 67–8
typology, 5, 81–2, 177

understanding, 162–3
United States of America, 20, 43, 44, 94–5
university, 123–4
usage, 8
uvula, 94, 177

variation, 4–5, 9, 54–5, 136–7; *see also* dialect; style; time
verb, 4, 5, 7, 25, 62–8, 72–3, 85–7, 110, 177
  auxiliary, 8, 22–4, 171
  irregular, 35
vocabulary, 33–4, 49–51, 55–6, 74, 85, 154–5
voice, 10–11, 62–3, 178
voiceless, 10–11, 178
vowel, 3, 58–9, 124, 178

wicket-keeper, 89
wife, 10
window, 10
word class, 74, 107–9; *see also* part of speech
word order, 5, 25, 74, 88, 107
world language, 138–40, 143–4
writing, 6–7, 8, 9, 38–9, 45–8, 53–4, 82, 149, 160

you, 70, 159

Zulu, 83, 100–5